Perthshire
in History
and Legend

ARCHIE McKERRACHER

JOHN DONALD PUBLISHERS LTD
EDINBURGH

For Angus, Ruari, Niall and Sarah Rose

ISBN 085976 223 8

Exclusive distribution in the United States of America
and Canada by Humanities Press Inc.,
Atlantic Highlands, NJ 07716, USA.

The cover photograph of the author is
by John A. Fraser Photography, Dunblane.

Phototypesetting by Pioneer Associates Ltd., Perthshire.
Printed in Great Britain by
Bell & Bain Ltd., Glasgow.

Acknowledgements

My thanks to the many people who have given freely of their time over the years, and without whose enthusiasm and interest this book could not have been written. They include Dukes and Earls; stalkers and shepherds; factors and folklorists; clan chiefs and clan historians; librarians of the Sandeman Library, Perth; the Scottish Room of the Edinburgh Central Library; the Mitchell Library, Glasgow; and the National Library, Edinburgh. Also the Archivists of Perth County, Canada; Central Regional Council and Perth District Council, Scotland.

My especial thanks to Pauline Leask for her work in deciphering my writing, correcting spelling, and typing the manuscript. Also for her advice and assistance and her unfailing cheerfulness.

Any errors and omissions in the text are mine alone.

Contents

Acknowledgements   iii
1. By Strathfillan and Killin   1
2. The Crooked Glen of Stones   32
3. The Curse of the Breadalbanes   61
4. In Balquhidder and the Trossachs   89
5. Around Doune and the Carse   114
6. The Devil, the Prince, and the Flower of Dunblane   140
7. From Ardoch to Almondbank   163
8. In the Heart of Strathearn   189
Index   206

CHAPTER 1

By Strathfillan and Killin

Twelve centuries ago, when Scotland was a dark and pagan land, there came here a missionary from Ireland. This was no ordinary priest, for his mother was Kentigerna, Princess of Leinster, while his father was Feradach, of the noble race of Fitiach Finn, and of the Royal House of Dalriada.

The saintliness of Fillan MacFeradach began early, for legends tell how he was born with a stone in his mouth — possibly a hair lip — and how his disappointed father hurled him into a pool to drown. He was brought safely to the shore by watching angels, and rescued by Bishop Ibar, who fostered him and brought him up in the Christian faith.

In time he was ordained as a monk, and accompanied by his mother he crossed from Ireland to Wester Ross around A.D. 703. Here they spread the Word of the Lord until Fillan decided to carry the faith to West Perthshire, where few missionaries had been before. This was a wild region which lay at the very extremity of the Scots Kingdom of Dalriada (Argyll), while to the east lay Pictland, and to the south was the kingdom of the Britons. He and his mother set out together, for she had resolved to found a nunnery on an island on Loch Lomond which is still called after her foundation, Inch Cailleach — The Island of the Old Women or Nuns. The journey was long and hard, but eventually they passed through what is now Argyll but was then a desolate, savage wilderness, and, assisted by Fillan's pastoral staff, they climbed to the top of the great watershed near Tyndrum where the waters flow east to the North Sea and west to the Atlantic. A few miles on and a fertile glen opened out, and Fillan sensed this was the place to begin his ministry. He chose a site for his cell beside the River Dochart, in the glen now known as Strathfillan.

Little is known of his work except that he became revered
throughout the countryside and regarded as a saint. More
and more of the local people left their pagan worship in the
hills and came down to listen and be baptised, and his tiny
church became renowned as a place of learning.

His miracles continued, and there is the story of the lay
brother who saw a light shining from the saint's cell one
night. He peered through a chink in the wall, and saw the
saint writing by means of a brilliant light which streamed
from his upheld left hand. Next day a tame stork plucked
out the eye of the prying man, but it was restored by the
saint. Another legend tells of his ploughing with a pair of
oxen when a wolf appeared and killed one of them. Fillan
knelt in prayer and the wolf meekly returned and allowed
itself to be yoked to the plough.

The Dewars of St. Fillan

As the years went by St. Fillan grew frail. He now walked
painfully with his treasured pastoral staff to his preaching
seat at Suie, in Glendochart. His life of missionary work in
this bleak spot had taken its toll, and it was apparent he was
dying. Shortly before his death in 777 A.D. he called to his
bedside five of his most faithful lay brothers, and charged
them with the keeping for all time of the precious symbols of
his work. This they promised to do, and in exchange they
were to be given a croft of land, and an annual gift of meal.

The relics they were to be given were St. Fillan's pastoral
staff, called the Coigerach; the Bell of St. Fillan, known as
the Bernane, or 'Little Capped One'; and the Fergy, the
Mayne, and the Meser. What the last three were is unknown
but it is suggested the Fergy was the saint's portable altar, the
Mayne was his armbone from which had come the miraculous
light, and the Meser was the manuscript he was writing.

These men were called in Gaelic, 'Deoradh', a word
originally meaning 'Pilgrim' or 'wanderer', probably because

St. Fillan established his monastic cell in Strathfillan after crossing over from Iona around 703 A.D.

they often carried the saint's relics far afield. Later, the meaning of the word altered to 'custodian', and the Gaelic word itself became modified into the modern surname of Dewar. Their duties in carrying the saint's relics into foreign parts were clearly stipulated. Any inhabitant of Glendochart who had cattle carried off could apply to the Dewar Coigerach with fourpence, or a pair of shoes, and food for the first night, and the Dewar was obliged to seek out the beasts 'wherever they might be found within the bounds of the Kingdom of Scotland' — according to evidence heard at an inquest in 1428.

By the twelfth century the saint's original cell had been enlarged into a small church the size of the present ruins, and had an abbot in charge. But probably by now it was a Roman church, for the old Celtic or Columban church had been suppressed during the reign of King Malcolm Canmore in the eleventh century. A sizeable monkish community existed here, and evidence of their life can still be seen. A short distance to the north is the Priests' Well, still enclosed by stonework, and about two hundred yards east of Kirkton Farmhouse are the remains of a rectangular wall enclosing the monks' garden. To the north of the church is a very old graveyard — evidence that a much older building stood on this site, for in Roman Catholic times that site was reserved for the Evil One, and suicides.

As the old Celtic Church was absorbed by the Roman, more and more land was removed from St. Fillan's chapel to other dioceses, and its influence waned. An Abbot still presided over it, and sanctuary was still provided for hunted men. The fugitive King Robert the Bruce came here in 1306, shortly after his coronation, and his tiny band rested under the thatched roof. To their Ard-Righ came the Dewars of the Coigerach and the Mayne, and gave him the Gaelic blessing of St. Fillan, much to the annoyance of the Abbot and Bishop Moray who frowned upon this Celtic ritual. The blessing of the Old Church proved highly efficacious for, shortly after leaving, the King's party was attacked by the McDougalls of Lorn, at nearby Dalrigh, and had a miraculous escape.

Both these Dewars were at the Battle of Bannockburn, and Boece relates that on the eve of battle the King knelt in prayer before the casket containing the Mayne. Suddenly there was a click and the case opened. The terrified Dewar looked inside, and whispered, 'Here is a great miracle'. He confessed to the King that he had left the relic behind in case it was lost, and now the saint's armbone had miraculously appeared. Fortified by this sign of divine approval, King Robert went on to win one of history's greatest victories.

The grateful monarch later made many gifts to the church in Strathfillan, and had it elevated into a priory, confirmed by Pope Clement VI in 1348.

The Dewars of St. Fillan are mentioned in many old records but, of course, always as a description of the person; surnames as such only came into use in the seventeenth and eighteenth centuries. The earliest account is a missive dated 1336 from Alexander Menzies, Lord of Glendochart, to

'Donald McSobrell, Dewar Cogerach', confirming him in the lands of Ewich in Strathfillan, and free from all taxes.

In 1428 an inquest was held before a jury by the Baillie of Glendochart to establish what privileges were attached to the custodian of the Coigerach or Quigrich, as it was sometimes called. They found that 'Finlay Jore (Doire or Dewar) should have for all time half a boll of meal from every inhabitant of Glendochart holding more than a half merkland of ground'. These rights were confirmed in 1487 by Royal Charter of James III in favour of one Malise Doir, and possibly the then custodian felt the necessity for this as the Church was casting covetous eyes at his possession.

The Prior of Strathfillan, Hew Currie, tried to obtain a decree in 1549 to compel 'Malise Doir of Quigrich, Archibald Doir of Fergy and Malcolm Doir of Bernane to deliver and present in the kirkis of Straphillan certain reliques, and nocht to be taken furth agane without the licence of the said prioure'. Failing this, the Dewars were to be excommunicated.

However, the Lords of the Council found in favour of the hereditary custodians, and absolved them from any punishment. Holy Church decided to seek revenge in other ways, and in 1551 Queen Mary issued an order assessing for tax 'Malise Dewar, the forty shilling land of Ewich . . . which have never been computed in any rental'.

Apparently at this time the five hereditary Dewars still held the land granted to them eight centuries before. Malise, Dewar Quigrich, had his croft at Ewich, near St. Fillan's church; the Dewar Bernane's croft was at Suie in Glendochart; the Dewar Fergy's croft was at Auchlyne, where stands the ruined Chapel Na Farig; the Dewar Meser had the lands of Corehynan; and the Dewar Mayne had a croft at Killin, still called today 'Croft na Dewar'.

The Dewars were regarded as the leading families in Strathfillan and Glendochart, and were a source of irritation to the established church, for the local people still used the relics in healing rituals which went back to pre-Christian times. However, the effect of land taxes, and the coming of the Reformation, eventually drove the Dewars from their lands. The line of Dewars of the Fergy, the Mayne and the Meser died out, and their relics were probably destroyed by zealous Reformers.

By the early seventeenth century the line of Dewar Bernane also failed, and St. Fillan's bell was removed to the graveyard of Strathfillan Church. Here it sat on top of a flat tombstone, supposedly the Saint's grave, exposed to the elements. It was venerated by the local people, who regarded it with superstitious awe, and the bell became the centrepiece of one of the strangest ceremonies ever enacted in the Highlands.

A mile upstream from the ruined priory lies the Holy Pool, overlooked by a hillock with three cairns on top. People flocked here from miles around to bathe in the water, which was supposed to cure all ailments.

An English visitor to Tyndrum in 1798 noted this curious healing ceremony, and recorded in his diary:

'August 9th, 1798. Arrived at Tyndrum by 4 o'clock. Rode after dinner with a guide to the Holy Pool of Strathfillan. Here again is abundant cause for talking of the superstition of the Highlanders. The tradition avers that St. Fillan, a human being, who was made a saint about the beginning of the eighth century by Robert de Bruce, consecrated this pool, and endued it with a power of healing all kinds of diseases, but more especially madness. This virtue it has retained ever since, and is resorted to by crowds of neighbouring peasantry, who either expect to be cured of real diseases, or suppose themselves cured of imaginary ones. This healing virtue is supposed to be most powerful towards the end of the first quarter of the moon, and I was told that if I had come there tomorrow night and the night after I should have seen hundreds of both sexes bathing in the pool. I met five or six who were just coming away from taking their dip, and amongst them an unfortunate girl out of her mind, who came for thirty miles distance to receive the benefits of the waters, and had been there for several

The remains of the early fourteenth-century chapel in Strathfillan founded here by Robert the Bruce as thanks for his victory at Bannockburn in 1314. It was built on the site of St. Fillan's eighth-century church and was used until last century for a curious healing ceremony.

months together, but had never derived the smallest advantage, and, indeed, she appeared so completely mad, that, whatever may be the virtue of St. Fillan's Pool, I am sure Willis would pronounce her a hopeless case.

'A rocky point projects into the pool. This pool is by no means the fountain head, for the water runs for a long way up the country, yet it is not supposed to receive its virtue till it comes to the very place, on the one side of which the men bathe, and on the other side the women. Strathfillan derives its name from the saint. Near Strathfillan a famous battle was fought between King Robert de Bruce and the MacDougalls, which the former gained owing to the assistance afforded by the prayers of St. Fillan.

'Each person gathers up nine stones in the pool and after bathing walks to a hill near the water, where there are three cairns, round each of which he performs three turns, at each turn depositing a stone, and if it is for bodily pain, a fractured limb, or sore that they are bathing, they throw upon one of the cairns that part of their clothing which covered the part affected; also if they have at home any beast that is diseased, they have only to bring some of the meal which it feeds upon, and make it into paste with these waters, and afterwards give it to him to eat, which will prove an infallible cure; but they must likewise throw upon the cairn the rope or halter with which it was led. Consequently, the cairns are covered with old halters, gloves, shoes, bonnets, night-caps, rags of all sorts, kilts, petticoats, garters, and smocks. Sometimes they go as far as to throw away their half-pence. Money has often been called the root of all evil, but for the disease of what part of the body these innocent half-pence are thus abused I could not learn. However, we may venture to suppose that they seldom remain there long without somebody catching the disorder again.

'When mad people are bathed they throw them in with a rope tied about the middle, after which they are taken to St. Fillan's Church, about a mile distant, where there is a large stone with a nick carved in it just large enough to receive them. In this stone, which is in the open Churchyard, they are fastened down to a wooden frame-work, and there remain for the whole night with a covering of hay over them, and St. Fillan's Bell is put upon their heads. If in the morning the unhappy patient is found loose, the saint is supposed to be very propitious. If, on the other hand, he continues in bonds, he is supposed to be contrary.

'The Bell is of very curious shape, and has an iron tongue. St. Fillan caused it to fly to this Church, and a soldier seeing it in the air, fired at it, which brought it down and occasioned a crack on it, which is still to be seen. I was told that wherever this Bell was removed to it would always return to a particular place in the Churchyard next morning. This Church had been formerly twice as large as it is now, as appears by the ruin of what has been pulled down, a striking proof of the desecration, either of the population, or religion in this country. In order to ascertain the truth of St. Fillan's Bell I carried it off with me to England. An old woman who observed what I was about asked me what I wanted with the Bell and I told her I had an unfortunate relation at home out of his mind, and that I wanted to have him cured. 'Oh, but,' she says, 'you must bring him here to be cured, or it will be of no use.' Upon which I told her he was too ill to be moved, and off I galloped with the Bell to Tyndrum Inn.'

The Bernane bell's homing instincts obviously did not work on foreign soil, for it remained in England for the next seventy years until a chance conversation between Bishop Forbes of Brechin and another guest at a country house in Hertfordshire in 1869. The stranger informed the Bishop that a relative held St. Fillan's bell, and immediate steps were taken for its recovery.

The relic is now on display in the National Museums of Scotland, in Edinburgh, where it can be seen to be an excellent example of a Celtic bronze bell, cast in one piece, and having the traditional wide mouth. But however unusual the story of St. Fillan's bell, that of his Quigrich, or pastoral staff, is even more remarkable.

At the time of the Reformation most of the Dewars were forced from their ancestral crofts with the exception of the Dewar Quigrich who remained until 1574. In that year, in a Charter of James VI, there is confirmation of the sale of the lands of Ewich from 'Donald Macindeara vic Cogerach,' or Donald, son of the Dewar, to Sir Duncan Campbell of Glenorchy. From that time the fortunes of the Dewars Quigrich began to wane. Around 1600 they sold the Quigrich to the Catholic McDonnells of Glengarry, who were delighted with such a relic. The sale only increased the Dewars' misfortune, and they never rested until they had repurchased

The Holy Pool on the River Dochart. Here sick people were brought to be cured.

the staff. A later Dewar confirmed his right of possession at the Court of Session in 1734, and lodged with his appeal the well-preserved letter his ancestor had received from James III.

Ill luck still followed the Dewars Quigrich, and in 1782 they were represented by Malise Dewar, a day labourer, who resided with his consumptive eldest son in a mean cottage in Grey Street, Killin. It was here that William Thompson, an Oxford graduate, saw the Quigrich, and wrote to the Earl of Buchan, president of the newly formed Society of Antiquaries of Scotland, suggesting they should purchase the staff. Unfortunately, the letter was overlooked and no action taken. A French tourist in 1795 was astonished to find that Presbyterians still travelled over a hundred miles to drink healing water that had been passed through the inside of the crozier.

After the death of Malise and his consumptive son, the relic passed to the younger brother, Alexander, who took it to Edinburgh in 1808, and advertised in the *Caledonian Mercury* that 'there is to be seen at the first entry below

Covenant Close a most curious antiquity, in the family of the proprietor since before the time of Robert the Bruce. Admittance two shillings'.

From this unscrupulous custodian the Quigrich passed to his son, Archibald, who had a farm in Balquhidder, and then Glenartney. Along with thousands of other farmers he was ruined in the agricultural depression that followed the Napoleonic Wars, and petitioned the Government for free passage and free land in Canada. He left Scotland in 1818, taking with him the treasured Quigrich, and settled in Beckwith, Ontario. His son, Alexander, followed him, but could not settle in this new country despite the fact that all around were Gaelic-speaking Perthshire Highlanders.

Eventually, he came to like his adopted country, married a Scots girl, and moved to the township of Plympton, Ontario, in 1850, taking with him the Quigrich which he had inherited. Here he prospered and raised a large family. Once again the Dewar Quigrich became a greatly respected person, and many Canadian Highlanders came to his farm seeking water passed through the staff to give to an ailing animal.

About this time a Scots Canadian priest, the Rev. Eneas McDonnell, a descendant of the McDonnells of Glengarry who had bought the Quigrich in the seventeenth century, discovered the saint's relic was held in a remote farmhouse on the Canadian prairies. He wrote to Dr. Daniel Wilson, Secretary of the Society of Antiquaries, and several attempts were made to buy the crozier. The Earl of Elgin, senior member of the Bruce family, offered £400 in 1859, but Alexander Dewar always refused.

Chance took Dr. Wilson to a post at Toronto University, and he established contact with the Dewar in 1870. The hereditary custodian was now 87, and worried that his sons would not have the same interest in preserving the saint's staff. He agreed to part with it for 700 dollars of which 200 dollars was to be his donation towards the acquisition. In 1876 Alexander Dewar, with the consent of his son Archibald, executed a deed of transfer to the Society, and gave the Quigrich 'on trust to deposit the same in the National Museum of Antiquities in Edinburgh, there to remain for all time to come for the use, benefit and enjoyment of the Scottish nation'. However, the hereditary title of Dewar Quigrich was to remain with the family to avoid any bad luck.

When the Quigrich was examined on its arrival in Edinburgh it was found to be a nine-inch-high head of a pastoral staff. The casing is of silver gilt with patterns of filigree around silver plaques. At the crook end is a small carved bust and inset charm stone, and the superb workmanship is of fourteenth-century origin. There was considerable puzzlement why some of the filigree appeared different than the rest, but when the outer casing was removed a much older crozier of the ninth century was found inside. Although the wood has long since disappeared, the bronze covering remains, and it was obvious this original staff had been stripped of all its ornamentation to decorate the outer casing.

In the days when St. Fillan used it as he spread the Word of God around the lonely glens it would have been a staff of rare and wonderful beauty.

Today this ancient relic of one of Scotland's most revered saints lies safely on display in the museum in Queen Street, Edinburgh. The present hereditary custodian is Thomas Douglas Battersby Rutherford Dewar, Dewar Coigerach, whose heraldic insignia bears two pastoral staves in saltire behind his arms. Those who pause to admire the rare beauty of the staff should remember the fidelity and devotion of the long line of Dewars Coigerach who, down through twelve hundred years, have faithfully carried out their promise to St. Fillan.

The Sons of the Abbot

When St. Fillan died in 777 A.D. his co-arb or heir was his

nephew Ferchar Og Abruaruadh, son of Fillan's brother, Ferchar Fada, 15th King of Dalriada. It was the custom of the Celtic Church to choose its Abbots from the Founder's Kin, for it was not a celibate order. Thus the old manuscripts trace twenty unbroken generations of hereditary Abbots of Glendochart from 777 to 1336. However, it seems more likely that a grandson of King Kenneth MacAlpine, Gillefilain (= servant of Fillan), was appointed Abbot in the late ninth century. From Gillefilain stem the Clan McGregor who were Lords of Glendochart and Glenlochy, and from him too stem later the Mac an abba (= the sons of the abbot). It would thus appear that Clan Gregor is the senior branch of the Siol Alpin (= the House of Alpin) and not the Macnabs as is often claimed.

The Macnabs

The name Mac an abba is first found in a Charter of 1124 in the reign of David I. Unfortunately, it is often misspelt today as MacNab which would mean the Son of Nab. In 1138 John de Glendochart witnessed a Charter granted to Malduin, third Earl of Lennox, and later the Abbot of Glendochart and the Earl of Atholl together governed part of Argyll. By this time the old Celtic abbacies had been completely secularised and the hereditary 'Sons of the Abbot' would have held on to the church lands as their personal property. In 1306 the head of the Macnabs, Angus, joined forces against Robert the Bruce to seek vengeance for the murder of his brother-in-law, the Red Comyn. The Macnab lands were forfeited and their writs burned after the battle of Bannockburn when King Robert exacted savage reprisals on his enemies. However, it appears Angus was of the House of Innisshewan, for in 1336 Gilbert Mac an abba of Bovain was granted a charter by David II, and the chiefs of the modern Clan Macnab are reckoned from him.

By 1500 the Macnabs had consolidated their estates until

these stretched from Tyndrum to beyond Killin. Their castle stood at Ellanrayene, or Eilean Ran, an island commanding the strategic Port of Ran at the mouth of the River Lochay at Killin, and from here the Macnabs held power over Loch Tay and Glendochart. In the fifteenth and sixteenth centuries their nearest neighbours to the south were the small Clan Neish. They descended from Ness, son of one William, who was Sheriff of Perth and Lord of Leuchars around 1100 A.D. Ness gave his sons land in Angus, Fife and Galloway, but to his youngest son, Math, he gave land in Strathearn. Here, far removed from the rest of the family, Math established a small, independent clan, and by 1250 A.D. their headquarters were in a keep on a crannog, or artificial island, at St. Fillans on Loch Earn.

They seem to have been an unruly and troublesome lot, for at a Council held at Linlithgow on January 9, 1490, James IV gave orders to Lord Drummond: 'Whin 15 dais fra this dai furth to ger cast doon ye hoose of ye Easter Isle of Loch Ern, and distroy all ye strengthis of ye samen, and tak away ye bate, and put her to ye Wester Isle [at Lochearnhead]'.

However, the MacNesses, or Neishes, as they were now called, still inhabited the ruins of their tower, and continued their unlawful activities mainly at the expense of their northerly neighbours, the Macnabs. The enmity between the clans grew stronger, and there was always fighting whenever isolated groups of clansmen encountered each other.

Then in the year 1522 the Neishes made a major raid on the Macnab herds. Finlay Macnab, 8th chief of the House of Bovain, summoned all his clan, and they marched over the hills from Loch Tay to Glen Boltachan. The Neishes were alerted, and they, too, summoned all their men and advanced up the glen carrying their banner of a cupid armed with bow and arrow. The site of the conflict was around a huge boulder on what is now Little Port Farm, and as the Macnabs rushed downhill they threw away their plaids and, naked apart from their brogues, flung themselves upon the Neishes. The Neishes threw off their plaids as well, and soon the glen was

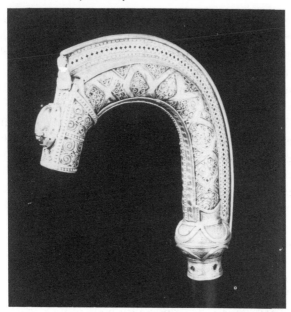

The Quigrich, or Crozier, of St. Fillan. The head is of fourteenth-century workmanship but incorporates silver filigree work from the original ninth-century head enclosed within. Photo: Royal Museum of Scotland.

packed with naked, screaming warriors locked in mortal combat.

The Neishes were no match for their adversaries and they fell like ninepins. The aged chief saw his three sons killed before his eyes. He retreated until he stood against the boulder and fought off his attackers with his claymore, which had a remarkable accessory in the shape of an iron ball which slid on a chain along the blade to give added weight to his blows. But the attackers were too many, and the old man finally succumbed to a hail of stabs from dirks and claymores. It is said that the unusual red lichen that covers the stone is still stained with the blood of the chief of Clan Neish.

The clan bard, and relation of the chief, MacCallum Glas, managed to drag away only twenty survivors to the island refuge on Loch Earn. During the next century their numbers increased little, and they were now little more than thieves and freebooters who preyed upon helpless travellers. However, they were no longer a major threat, and they might have continued with their way of life but for a dreadful error in the year 1612.

The Macnabs' Revenge

The story of their fearful mistake and its savage aftermath is found in many books. How the Neishes seized the Macnab chief's Christmas supplies, and how he called his twelve sons together and uttered the cryptic words 'Tonight is the night, if the lads were the lads!' The twelve sons then rowed a boat down to Ardeonaig on Loch Tay and lifted it from the water to carry it overland to Loch Earn. They surprised the Neishes, cut off their heads and returned with them to Ellanrayne Castle. Their delighted father exclaimed 'Tonight *was* the night! and the lads *were* the lads!', and his sons proudly handed over the gory heads to their mother, suggesting she give them to the younger children as playthings.

This is the version of the story as it appears in most books but certain aspects are conflicting. Why, for instance, should the Macnab chief say to his sons 'Tonight is the night. . . .'? These almost contemptuous words are hardly those a proud father would use to his grown-up sons who had already proved their manhood. Why again do the books say that twelve sons took part when the clan crest portrays a boat with only four oars? Why should the sons have taken the long overland route from Ardeonaig on Loch Tay to St. Fillan's on Loch Earn? A Black Watch T.A. exercise 'John Macnab', carried out in 1968, proved it was impossible to carry even a light coracle by this route in under eight hours. Lastly, it seems highly improbable, even in those violent times, that the sons would present severed heads to their mother with the suggestion that the younger children play with them.

Unfortunately, all the clan records were destroyed when Ellanrayne Castle was burnt by Cromwellian troops, and this, coupled with a gap of more than three centuries, makes it difficult to unravel the true story. However, much new evidence has come to light, particularly through the researches of the late Archibald Corrie Macnab, 22nd Chief, and research in other areas convinces me that the real story was as follows.

Just before Christmas of 1612 the Chief of the Clan Macnab had despatched his servants to Crieff to bring back food and drink for the festive season. The laden line of ponies was returning slowly by way of Comrie when the party was suddenly surprised and ambushed by the Neishes. There was great rejoicing when it was discovered who the goods were destined for, and the Neishes gleefully carried them off to Loch Earn.

As they were nearing the shore they were suddenly confronted by an aged crone who lived nearby. She was reputed to be a witch, being wild of face and deformed, and the Neishes respectfully saluted her and offered her a share of the plunder. She rejected it, pointed her finger at the Neishes' moored boat, then raised her arms to the sky and cried out, 'Beware, sons of Ness, beware of the time when there will be *two* boats on Loch Earn'.

The Neishes looked at each other uneasily, then remembered that they owned the only boat on the loch, and burst out laughing. They conveyed the goods across to their island in the boat, while the remainder used the secret causeway of boulders that can still be seen in line with the islet and the villa called 'Portmore' at St. Fillans.

Meanwhile the Macnab servants had reached Ellanrayne Castle and gasped out the story to Finlay Macnab, 12th Chief of the Clan. Finlay had married twice. His first wife was Katherine Campbell, the natural daughter of Sir Duncan

Loch Earn from above St. Fillans. In the foreground is the island where the Clan Neish had its hideout, and where they were destroyed by the sons of MacNab. The ruins of their castle can still be seen. In the background is the glen down which the MacNabs carried their boat after bringing it overland from Loch Tay.

Campbell of Glenorchy, and she had borne him two sons and a daughter. The name of his second wife is unknown, but she gave him ten sons. This lady, on hearing the story, suddenly saw an opportunity of removing her two stepsons, and making her own children the heirs. She looked at the eldest, Iain *Min* ('Smooth John') and sneeringly remarked, 'Tonight is the night — if the lads were the lads!'

She knew the fierce pride of Iain *Min* — a giant of a man who was nicknamed Smooth because he was anything but that — and knew that her words would goad him into hasty action. They did. Iain *Min* leapt to his feet shouting for his brother Duncan to arm himself. His two eldest half-brothers, John Roy and Patrick, also demanded to go, and their mother bit her lip but dare not refuse. Iain *Min* brushed aside his father's protests that the entire clan should be called out, and the brothers hurried to the lochside and unmoored their skiff. From here they rowed down Loch Tay to Cloichran where they hoisted the boat from the water on to their shoulders, and began the long trek up the side of Alt Breaclaich to the lochan at the top.

Gasping and staggering in the deep snow, they climbed over the saddle and down across the desolate plateau that leads to Glen Tarken. The descent down the steep, boulder-strewn glen was severe, but by the middle of the night they had launched their boat on Loch Earn.

The moon shone fitfully from behind scudding clouds as they rowed stealthily towards the island. Quietly they steered their craft into a tiny creek from where they could see a glimmer of light from the ruin. They crept up to a straw-filled window and peered inside. There lay the entire gang, gorged and drunk, and on a chair, snoring, the uncouth elderly chief. The four sons of Macnab made their way round the ruin to the makeshift door where Iain *Min* drew his dirk, and hammered on the wood.

'Who knocks?' called out the sleepy voice of the MacNeish chief. Iain *Min* replied in true Highland manner with another question: 'Who would you least like to see?'

There was a drunken laugh from inside. 'Smooth John Macnab!'

'Smooth John it is, but you'll find him a rough man tonight!' shouted Iain *Min* as he kicked the door open. The brothers rushed inside and began slaughtering all that were there — except for a boy and girl who cowered in terror under the table and were overlooked. Iain *Min* cut off the head of Chief of Clan Neish and instructed his brothers to cut off several others. With the heads stuffed in a sack, they set out on the long journey home.

They rowed back up Loch Earn, and, pulling the boat from the water, struggled up Glen Tarken, probably stopping to rest at the giant monolith that lies a short distance up the glen. From here it was a lung-wracking climb to the head of the glen. Eventually they could carry the boat no further and left it in the heather.

Then they hurried on and down to Loch Tayside, to make their way along the shore to Ellanrayne Castle.

About mid-morning they arrived back, to be greeted by their anxious father.

'Dread nought!' cried out Iain *Min* — an expression that is now part of the clan slogan.

His stepmother appeared, looking disappointed, and the chief turned to her and said in delight, 'Tonight *was* the night — and the lads *were* the lads!'

She enquired what was in the sack, and Iain *Min* gave her a cold stare.

'Bowls for your bairns!' he said, and opened the bag and rolled out the heads at her feet.

The girl who had hidden under the table during the massacre was the daughter of the Neish chief, and she eventually married the Laird of Torwood in Stirlingshire. The boy made his way to South Perthshire where he settled. The MacIldowie families in this area are descended from him — their name meaning 'Son of the Black-haired Lad'.

The Macnabs' boat lay rotting in the heather high up on the watershed between Loch Tay and Loch Earn, and is said to have been still visible around 1900. All traces of it were destroyed in a peat fire early this century, although a walking-stick made from the keel is said to be still in existence.

Other relics of that savage deed still survive, for the head of the Neish and the Boat appear on the Macnab Coat of Arms granted by the Lord Lyon King of Arms later that century, as does the motto 'Dreadnought-*Timor Omnis Abesto*', taken from the shout of triumph with which Iain *Min* greeted his father.

Iain *Min* later fought for Montrose and was captured while defending Kincardine Castle. He was condemned to death, but escaped from Edinburgh Castle. In 1651 he fought for Charles II at the Battle of Worcester along with three hundred of the clan. He returned home, but was killed in

1653 in a skirmish with Cromwellian troops who were raiding his cattle. The following year Ellanrayne Castle was burnt to the ground and the chiefs moved their seat to Kinnell House on the other side of the River Lochay.

The Great Macnab

The Macnabs were never a strong or large clan and their small estate suffered badly during the Civil Wars of the seventeenth century. The fortunes of the chiefs began to decline but one of the later chiefs became a legend in his own lifetime and is still a legend today.

He was Francis Macnab, sixteenth chief of Clan Mac an abba, of whom a contemporary wrote — 'Goliath of Gath, Caesar, Alexander, the Great Mogul — all were insignificant beside The Macnab!' And indeed they were, for Francis was the beau-ideal of a Highland chief and one of the Lords of Creation. He was born in Kinnell House in 1734, into a world little changed in six centuries, for the chief's word was still law and he ruled omnipotently, dispensing both justice and benevolence to his people. A Highland chief was an absolute monarch of his own little kingdom.

But on 16th April, 1746, the howl of grapeshot and the roar of cannon signalled the end of the old clan system as Prince Charles Edward's doomed attempt to restore the Stuarts to the throne was finally crushed on the sleet-sodden Moor of Culloden. A badly frightened Hanoverian Government in London ordered the Highland Chiefs to be stripped of all their power, and extended the reach of central authority and law into the mountains.

Francis Macnab was 54 when he succeeded his father as Chief in 1788. He had seen many of his fellow chiefs forced to sell their ancient lands through poverty. He had seen others turned into more landlords, aping the manners of the southern gentry, and treating their clansfolk as tenants rather than kin. Later they would clear their people from the land and replace them with sheep.

But Francis, or Francie, as he was affectionately known, refused to accept that the world had changed. He still maintained the traditions and honours of a chief of old. His tiny estate could scarcely support his lifestyle, but what proud chief ever demeaned himself by worrying about money? Who would dare demand payment from the Macnab? Was it not an honour for the tradespeople that he condescended to place an order with them? His debts began to mount and, to his consternation and outrage, his creditors began resorting to the new fangled courts of law.

When the bailiffs began to press, Francis would simply slip away to Kinnell House where an efficient army of informers allowed him to escape to the hills. One bold Sheriff's Officer once slipped through the net and found the Macnab in residence. Francis greeted him expansively and personally led him to the dinner table where he was plied with food and drink. The ghillies fussed around him, making the man feel embarrassed at having to raise the matter of unpaid bills in the morning. The bailiff awoke next morning and peered bleary-eyed from the window. To his horror he saw a body swinging by its neck from a tree. His anguished shout brought a servant running. 'Wha-what's that?' cried the man, pointing with a shaking hand. 'Oh, chust a messenger body who had the impertinence to serve a summons on the laird', came the casual reply. The wretch was out of the house in a flash, and riding hard back down the road to civilisation. Behind him the straw-filled dummy was cut down from the tree amidst howls of laughter, and no debt collector ever again dared pester Macnab at his home.

Francis was of mighty build, six foot three in height and of Herculean strength. His fine, romantic appearance made many a lady succumb to his charms, and his feats in this field became renowned. He never married, although Janet Buchanan of Leny raised an action against him in 1792 for having gone through a declaration of marriage with her. He

Francis Macnab, 'The Great Macnab', was the *beau ideal* of a Highland Clan Chief. He lived life as his ancestors had done despite his debts. Raeburn painted him in 1806 when Francis was 72, and his famous portrait captures the pride and arrogance of a Highland Chief with his foot on his native heath. Photo: Messrs Dewars Ltd.

was cleared by the court although many suspected he had indeed married the lady. It was during this case that the opposing counsel made a slighting reference to Francis as being the father of one hundred children. Francis rose to his full majestic height, purple with fury. 'Ye lying Deevil', he roared, 'I havnae!' 'Come, come, Macnab', said the Sheriff. 'It's common knowledge you must have at least ninety children'. 'Aye, ninety, maybe, my Lord', replied Francis quite seriously, 'but no' a hundred!'

Macnab's porridge cart is still remembered in Killin today. This used to set out from Kinnell every morning and stop at many a door along the High Street dispensing oatmeal for the laird's bairns. On one occasion Francis was passing through a hamlet far up Loch Tayside when he saw two little, red-haired boys fighting in the dust. 'Now, now, my lads', cried Macnab, as he separated them, 'Why are ye fechtin'?' One of the fighters brushed a tear from his eye. 'He says he's the son of the Chief', he sobbed, 'and I say I'm the son of the Chief'. 'Laddies, laddies, dinna fecht', said Francis kindly. 'Ye're *baith* the sons of the Chief!'

Many of the sons of Macnab became soldiers and fought with distinction all over the world, including two who fought at Waterloo. Francis did once almost marry legally and pressed his suit with the beguiling offer that the lady would be laid to rest 'in the most beautiful burial ground in the world' — the ancestral island burial place of the Chiefs on Inchbuie at Killin. The lady politely declined the offer.

Francis' amazing capacity for drink made him renowned even in an age noted for heavy drinking. He delighted in offering hospitality to one and all at his dinner table. However, he would deliberately seat himself in the lowliest place. A gentleman of noble birth once asked why Francis should so demean himself. Francis stared at him gravely. 'Wherever Macnab sits *is* the head of the table', he replied. His dinners would begin with the guests already convivial from ample refreshments. As the meal wore on, and more drink flowed, the conversation grew more garrulous but Macnab sat in silence gravely surveying the gathering. After a flask or two of whisky had slipped down his throat he would utter a few general remarks. After one or two more he began to warm up. When the meal was finished a huge, eight-gallon earthenware jug called The Batchelor was placed at his elbow. This contained whisky from his own distillery which he proceeded to pour down his throat in startling quantity. Now that he was relaxed he proceeded to make sweeping statements about anything and everything, particularly the ancestry of some of his fellow Chiefs. He denounced many as mere upstarts whose line went no further

Kinnell House at Killin, built about 1620, the ancestral home of the chiefs of Clan Macnab. It was bought in 1828 by the 1st Marquis of Breadalbane after the 17th Chief of Macnab fled to Canada to avoid bankruptcy. From 1940 to 1948 it was the home of the 9th Earl of Breadalbane, until repurchased in 1948 by Archibald Corrie Macnab, 22nd Chief, when the Campbells of Glenorchy and Breadalbane left the district for good.

back than four centuries. He dismissed the Hanoverian royal dynasty as mere mushrooms, and unfavourably compared the lineage of the royal families of Europe with his own. As Macnab steadily came into his own his guests slowly collapsed one by one onto the floor. A small boy was positioned beneath the table to loosen their collars and make them comfortable. Finally, the last surviving guest would slip floorwards with a groan. Francis would sorrowfully survey the scene of carnage, and give a slow shake of his head before marching steadily up to bed. The ghillies would then remove the unconscious guests.

Francis had founded a distillery to use up surplus barley

but unfortunately the authority of the Customs and Excise was beginning to spread into even Macnab's territory. He was the local Justice of the Peace and the excisemen ground their teeth in fury as he found one way or another to dismiss cases brought against operators of illicit mountain stills. A party of senior excisemen once came from the Lowlands to remonstrate with him. Macnab looked at them stonily. 'Excisemen!' he exclaimed with disgust, 'so ye're excisemen! There was once a cratur called Exciseman sent up here but — they killt him!'

Francis was also a colonel in the Royal Breadalbane Volunteers. In this capacity he was leading his troops to a review at Stirling when they were stopped by the excisemen who had information that the baggage carts were loaded with illicit whisky — which was true enough. Francis was clad in full uniform, complete with large silver buttons and buckles. Three tall, eagle's feathers fluttered from his bonnet and a large claymore hung by his side. He was an awesome and terrifying sight. 'Hounds! Vermin!', he roared. 'Wad ye dare stop His Majesty's officers and men on their way to fight for King and country? Ah, I kent it. Ye're Frenchies!' He turned to his men and shouted in Gaelic, 'My lads, this is likely to be a critical business. Load with ball!' The horrified excisemen took one look and fled for their lives.

Francis made many excursions to Edinburgh, reluctantly putting aside his kilt and dressing in old-fashioned clothes topped off with an ancient three-cornered hat. His refusal to accept the modern world and his proud bearing mixed with genteel poverty made him a legend in Edinburgh society. Many, of course, were not immediately aware of his standing. One miserable shopkeeper had the temerity to address him as 'Mr. Macnab'. Francis erupted with fury, his massive body shaking with anger, as he bellowed at the cowering man, 'By the saul of the Macnab, sir, naethin' but ye're diabolical Lowland ignorance can excuse ye for sic damnable profanation. There were, questionless, mony *Maister* Macnabs but the Auld Black Lad may hae my saul if I ken but ae *Macnab*!'

The story was often told of how Francis and his faithful servant took up residence in a fashionable Edinburgh hotel. They were shown into the best room where Francis surveyed the imposing four poster bed in silence. Then he ordered Donald to lift him up into the canopy, this being the only suitable position for a mighty chief. Donald climbed into the bed below and was soon snoring blissfully. He was awakened an hour later by his chief's imperious voice. 'Are ye comfortable down there, Donald?' he enquired. 'Oh aye, Macnab', replied Donald, 'I've nivir slept in sic a fine, feather bed.' There was a groan from above. 'Donald, if it wasna for the honour of the thing I hae a mind to come down and join ye!' Edinburgh became used to the sight of the now ageing Macnab reeling down Princes Street clad in his ancient finery, superbly portrayed in Kay's *Edinburgh Portraits*. But the town dandies had soon learned the folly of making fun at Macnab's expense. He appeared once at Musselburgh races riding a horse which had seen better days. 'I say, Macnab', cried out a wit. 'Would that be the same horse I saw you on last year?' 'Naw', replied Macnab, 'but it's the same whup!', and he lashed the insolent youth around the shoulders with his crop.

But as Francis grew older his debts steadily increased. Despite founding the Dreadnought Hotel at Callander, and several other successful business ventures, he was forced to part with his mother's estate at Arnprior. He continued to live life to the full without regard to his income, and paid his bills by issuing worthless paper notes on a Perthshire bank. They humoured the old Chief by accepting them, hoping to recover the money after his death.

Francis had named his nephew Archibald, born in 1788, as his heir. Archibald had been sent to London to train as a lawyer but he too spent his allowance unwisely. He invited Macnab to visit him in 1800 when Francis was 66. His nephew had prepared London for his arrival with many elaborate stories, and society flocked to meet him. They were not disappointed for Francis had lost none of his imposing

The branch which grafted into the trunk of another tree on the Macnabs' island burial ground of Inchbuie at Killin when their lands were sold in 1828. The graft died when the 22nd Chief of Clan Macnab recovered the ancestral estate in 1948.

appearance. He confirmed their belief that a Highland Chief was an autocrat in a democratic world, and a romantic figure. Francis and Archibald, both trying to impress, became involved in gambling where the stakes were far above their means. They visited a fashionable cock-fighting pit in Fleet Street where a powerful cock was defeating all opponents. Francis' booming voice echoed round the room. 'Aye, a guid bird and a fine fechter but I wager a bird frae Scotland wad kill it ony day.' 'A thousand guineas on it, sir', cried a dandy. Macnab blanched but continued boldly, 'I hae in mind a cock bird born and bred in Killin. A bird that would murder yon chicken.' 'I say, sir', cried another dandy, 'I'll wager two thousand guineas!' These were impossible amounts to

Macnab but he declared boldly, 'Name the day, sir, name the day'.

A date was set for a month hence, during which Francis returned home to find his cock. All London was agog with the challenge, and on the appointed day the pit was crowded with elegant dandies anxious to see the bold Highlander receive his come-uppance.

The English bird was released into the ring and strode around arrogantly, looking powerful and fierce with its spurred feet. 'There, sir, is The Pride of Lambeth', cried its owner. 'The finest bird in England. Now let's see this Scotch bird.' Francis came slowly forward positively glowing with whisky, and carrying a large basket which he set down in the ring. He tipped it open, and out stepped a mighty, furious and hungry cock eagle from Ben Lawers. Its eyes glowed red with anger and it was positively spitting with rage. The English bird took one look and with a frightened squawk tried to leap from the pit. A howl of protest went up. 'Wad ye insult the honour of Macnab?', roared Francis. 'Was it no a cock ye stipulated? In the Highlands we're accustomed to bring the best bird we can find. And besides,' he added, looking down with a beam, 'The Killin cock has jist eaten the Pride of Lambeth!'

It was during this London visit that Francis met the famous Scottish painter, Henry Raeburn. Raeburn had not yet achieved his later fame but he saw in Francis the ideal portrait of a Highland Chief of old. He decided to wait until he could paint Macnab amongst his native hills, and it was 1806 before the famous portrait was executed. Francis was then aged 72 and a battered giant, but Raeburn captured all the arrogance and pride of a Highland Chief with his foot on his native heath and monarch of all he surveyed. The painting shows Francis in the full uniform of a colonel of the Breadalbane Volunteers and is one of the finest portraits ever done. It seems more than appropriate that it now hangs in the London offices of the famous whisky firm of Dewars.

Francis Macnab died at Callander in 1816 aged 84. He

protested violently on his deathbed when the doctor refused
him as much whisky as he pleased. He approached death
laughing and joking, and telling scandalous stories from his
rich life, until his massive frame gave a tremble and then was
still. Francis Macnab, sixteenth Chief of Macnab, the last
survivor of the chiefs of old and born two centuries out of
time, finally passed to his Maker. He was carried home to
Killin in a huge oak coffin and laid to rest in the Chief's
enclosure on the island of Inchbuie.

The then modern world may have made allowances for
their beloved Francie but they made none for the new Chief,
Archibald, who had inherited the chieftainship and thirty-
five thousand pounds of debt. Archibald held off his creditors
for seven years until 1823 when he just slipped away one day
and fled to Canada, leaving behind a wife and six children
whom he never saw again. In Canada he tried to emulate his
late uncle and so impressed the authorities that he was
granted eighty-five thousand acres along the valley of the
River Ottawa. He made it into a personal estate and called it
'Macnab', and built a log house named 'Kinnell'. He founded
the town of Arnprior and persuaded many of the clan to
come over and settle. Several hundred came, only to find the
promises of assistance and food were never kept. They were
oppressed by Archibald who treated them as tenants and
forced them to work for him. Eventually a complaint was
made and the Canadian Government forced Archibald to
recompense the settlers to the tune of thirty-five thousand
pounds. He was a broken man and left Canada in 1853 for
the Orkneys where he lived on a small allowance from his
wife. He moved to Lannion in north-west France where he
died in 1860, aged 83. In an unmarked grave in that foreign
spot lies the last laird of the direct line of the House of
Bovain, Chiefs of Clan Macnab since 1336.

The Prophecy of the Grafted Pine

There is an extraordinary story attached to the downfall of

the Clan Macnab. In the seventeenth century there lived on Loch Tayside a remarkable seer called The Lady of Lawers. Around 1680 she uttered the prediction that *The lands of Macnab will be joined to those of Breadalbane when two trees join together on Inchbuie and grow as one.* In 1828, when the 1st Marquis of Breadalbane bought the bankrupt Macnab estate, there was a great storm which tore off a branch of a pine tree on the Macnab's ancestral burial island of Inchbuie. This was hurled many feet through the air until it came to rest against the trunk of another pine on the south side of the island. The dislodged branch grafted on to its new parent, although this is said to be botanically impossible, and the two grew and flourished as one during all the long years the Breadalbane family held the Macnab lands. The strange thing is that the graft withered and died in 1948 when Archibald Corrie Macnab, 22nd Chief, repurchased the ancestral estate from the ninth Earl of Breadalbane. On his death Kinnell House passed to his nephew, James Macnab of Macnab, 23rd Chief, who unfortunately has had to part with Kinnell and the estate in recent years. The Macnab still lives close by but is now the only one bearing that name in the old clan lands. Kinnell House with its four-foot thick walls dates back to the seventeenth century and was once noted for its Black Hamburgh vine, planted in 1832, and at one time 190 feet long and thought to be the biggest in the world. All that remains to the clan today is the ancestral burial island of Inchbuie with its enclosure containing the graves of fifteen Chiefs of Clan Mac an abba.

CHAPTER 2

The Crooked Glen of Stones

Twelve castles Fionn had,
In the Crooked Glen of Stones.
(From an epic Gaelic poem attributed to Ossian)

To the Gaelic speaker there is only one Gleann Dubh nan
Garbh Clach — The Crooked Glen of Stones — and that is
Glen Lyon in Perthshire. This beautiful, long, and twisting
glen runs over thirty miles from Weem, near Aberfeldy, to
the road-end at the foot of the mountains of Mamlorn.

Its Gaelic name, however, does not derive from the many
boulders, or the stark mountains that loom above, but from
the remarkable circular stone towers that are scattered along
its length, and which tradition associates with the legendary
hero, Fionn MacCumhaill, Fin MacCool or Fingal, and his
warrior band of the Fianna.

Until quite recent times, when a traveller in the glen
sought shelter, the first question his host would ask was
'Bheil dad agad air na Fiann?' — 'Can you speak of the days
of Fionn?' — and the whole family would listen for his reply,
hoping for a long evening of epic stories.

The tales and legends of Fionn and his followers are not,
of course, solely confined to these parts, but are found almost
everywhere in the Highlands. Some of the names and deeds
of the heroes are remembered in the numerous Fingal's
Caves; the Cuillins of Skye; the Gulf of Corryvreckan;
Ossian's Grave in the Sma' Glen; Killin, whose name means
Fionn's Grave; and many others. In Glenshee, and also in
Kintyre, is pointed out the site of the tomb of the beautiful
Diarmid for whom Fingal's wife developed a fatal passion.
After a great boar hunt her husband lured him to stand on
the back of the huge beast to measure it, and he was fatally

poisoned by a venomous bristle. From him is supposed to have descended Eva O'Duine, who married Gillespic Cam Beul, or 'Wry Mouth', to found the great Clan Campbell with its Gaelic name of Siol Diarmid, and its boar's head crest.

But wherever the great deeds were performed, it was Glen Lyon that was the legendary home of Fionn, and his Nine Thousand Warriors — the Host of the Fianna — the flower of Highland chivalry. The remains of their twelve towers are still to be seen in the glen with their adjacent moot-hills, or meeting mounds. Near these were the Testing Stones, which consisted of a heavy, rounded boulder with a flat stone behind it higher up. A recruit to the Fianna was not accepted till he had proved his manhood by lifting up the lower stone, and setting it on the other. Only one set of these Testing Stones still exists. It stands in a field opposite the House of Camusvrachan, midway along the glen.

Further up, near the hamlet of Cashlie (Castles), is the Bhacain, or Dog Stake, where the Fians tied their staghounds after hunting. This curiously-shaped stone on a mound near the road is about two feet high; whether it is man-made or otherwise is unknown. To this stake would be tethered Fionn's own dog, the mighty Bran, with its yellow paws, black flanks, and chain of pure gold. It was the best hunting dog that ever lived. Beside it was the dreaded Grey Hound that used to roam the Great Glen tearing its victims limb from limb, until it too became a Hound of the Fians. The dogs' food was tossed to them from the top of Caisteal Coin Bhacain — the Castle of the Dog Stake — nearly seventy yards away, and any hound that failed to catch its dinner was turned out of the pack!

These twelve forts in Glen Lyon are not the only ones associated with the Fians, for in an area stretching forty miles from the glen to Pitlochry, and fourteen from Blair Atholl to Amulree, are over forty of these curious circular stone towers. They effectively block every mountain pass or glen entrance, and yet, apart from five in the glen itself, none stands on a defensive site. Instead they are placed on low ground along valley floors, sometimes singly, sometimes in groups of two or three, while on the north side of Loch Tummel over fourteen lie close to each other.

These towers are unique, and quite different from the hundreds of hill forts that are dotted all over Scotland. Their construction, and groupings, are complicated and highly sophisticated, resembling very closely the brochs of Caithness and Orkney, except that in North Perthshire the towers were very much larger. An average tower had an internal diameter of eighty feet, two walls of hand-pitched stone about ten feet apart infilled with loose rubble, and a probable height of twenty feet. The best remaining example is Caisteal an Duibhe at the roadside near Cashlie. This incorporates a huge ten-foot-high boulder, and as the inner wall rises up to meet it the inference is that the walls were originally very much higher. Inside the towers would be various chambers, steps leading to the top, and a narrow access passage. The manpower expended to build them must have been immense for there is one on Pitlochry Golf Course that has an incredible diameter of one hundred and seven feet.

Only a few of the Fingalian towers are still recognisable, but of these, three in Glen Lyon near Cashlie still have Fingalian names associated with them: Caisteal an Dearg, or the Castle of Dargo, one of Fionn's captains; Caisteal an Dubh, or Castle of the Black (Hero); and Caisteal Coin nam Bhacain, the Castle of the Dog Stake. These towers may well be the oldest fortifications in Britain to which any definite tradition is attached.

But the strange thing is that Fhionn MacCumhaill, or Fingal, and the Fians, never existed in Scotland at all. The legends of a mercenary band of heroic warriors were imported from Ireland by the Dalriadic Scots when they arrived in Argyll from Ulster around 500 A.D. Three hundred years later, when they had moved east to rule all Scotland, the tales were grafted onto the old Pictish culture by the

The Testing Stones at Camusvrachan prove too heavy for the writer's young son. They were probably used as a test of physical strength.

Bards after the overthrow of the Pictish kingdom in 847 A.D. The stories became consolidated into a standard form between 1100 and 1400 A.D., and then in 1762 the publication by James Macpherson of supposedly undiscovered Gaelic poetic manuscripts under the title of 'The poems of Ossian' gave the seal of approval to the tales as part of actual Scottish history.

How, then, did a collection of Irish folk legends, which share a common root with the 'Tales of King Arthur' and the Hindu 'Ramayana', become so firmly associated with Scotland that even place-names, which change little, still recall the days of the fictitious Fianna? And who built the 'Forts of Fionn', and for what purpose? Why were over forty of these stone towers, with their unusual and advanced design, grouped together in a remote part of Highland Perthshire, and why, too, should this area have been selected as the home of the 'Fianna'? Was there something in the Pictish history to which the Bards of the Scots conquerors could conveniently attach their own Irish legends, and thus submerge the old Pictish culture into a common one? If so, then they succeeded admirably, for the master race of Picts is now a lost nation.

To seek an answer it is necessary to examine the history of the Picts, or what is known of it. It is believed this mysterious race entered Scotland from Scandinavia, and gradually absorbed the native people. The nickname of Picti, or Painted Ones, was given to them by the Romans who had good reason to fear this warlike race who steadily drove them back to behind Hardian's Wall. By the sixth century A.D. the Picts were divided into two separate kingdoms of northern and southern tribes, one called the Orc, or Boar Clan, which had entered through Orkney, and moved down to the south, the other the Cat Clan that had come through the Moray Firth, remaining there but also pushing north to Caithness and Sutherland.

The kingdoms were divided by The Mounth, the great range of mountains that includes the Grampians, and runs from Inverness to Loch Lomond. Although the two dynasties were later united, it is an interesting thought that a thousand years later a Clan of the Boar (Clan Campbell) fought for the last time against Clans of the Cat (McIntoshes, Farquharsons, Macphersons, etc.) at the Battle of Culloden Moor.

In 503 A.D. the Dalriadic Scots invaded Western Pictland, or Argyll, and pushed back the Picts to the mountain line of Drum Albain. Later, two other nations threatened from the south — the Britons of Strathclyde whose capital was Dumbarton, and whose territory extended from North Wales to Glen Falloch, and the Angles of Northumbria. The latter nation, under King Oswyn of Bernicia, attacked Pictland in the mid-sixth century, and occupied the southern part of the kingdom as far as The Mounth for thirty years. Then arose a great leader of the Picts, King MacBride, who united the entire nation, and defeated the invader at Nechtansmere, near Forfar, driving him back to the line of Forth and Clyde.

Thus a map of Scotland at the beginning of the seventh century A.D. would show the western boundary of Pictland lying along the great spine of the Drum Albain mountains, from the Great Glen to Glen Falloch. Two potential enemies, Scots and Britons, lay on either side of the apex of a triangle of which Glen Lyon forms the point, and later, a third, the Vikings, were to threaten from the north-west. Thus a modern Ordnance Survey map reveals that the twelve 'Forts of Fionn' in the glen are situated at the foot of mountain passes that give speedy access to almost every part of the Pictish boundary. The map also explains the reason why only five out of forty towers were built on high ground. Three of these, high up on the mountains of Mamlorn at the head of the glen, command the outlook to the south, west and north. The other two guard the narrow entrance to the glen at its foot: one on Drummond Ridge (The Ridge of Fionn), while perched on a crag directly opposite is Dun Geal, above Fortingall. Its name is also associated with Fionn, and with the traditional birthplace of Pontius Pilate, and for this reason will be dealt with later. Some archaeologists suggest these were ring forts and defensive homesteads occupied by pastoralists who perhaps came here from the west under the protection of an early Christian mission.

Carbon dating of charcoal taken from one of these structures indicates a date of seventh to tenth century A.D. However, after taking all the evidence into account, it is my belief that these 'Fingalian' Forts were instead part of a sophisticated military defence system which was in use until the overthrow of the Pictish kingdom in 847 A.D. There was indeed a Fianna, or Feinne (Followers; Warriors; Heroes) but it was not composed of the legendary Irish Heroes. Instead it was the army of the Pictish Kings, and Glen Lyon and the surrounding area was its mustering and training ground. Traditionally, the Pictish nation was divided into seven Provinces, six of which were ruled by a Maormer, or local king, and composed of Tuaths, or tribes, each commanded by a Toiseach, or Captain. The seventh Province, of which Glen Lyon forms part, was Fortrenn (Men of the Earn), which was the personal property of the High King of Picts. It remained the possession of later successive monarchs until Robert the Bruce gave away much of it to his loyal supporters. From this organisation comes the traditional title of the kings of Scotland — the Ard Righ, or High King — and from Toiseach, too, comes the modern name of MacIntosh.

The stone towers in the Glen Lyon area must have been known to the early and rather biased writer, Gildas, when he wrote in 570 A.D. of 'Swarthy columns of vermin from their small caverns of narrow outlet, loathsome hoards of Picts'. Nowhere else in Scotland merits this description, and it is my belief that Glen Lyon was the citadel of the regular army of the Pictish High Kings — his Feinne of the Men of Earn. The towers further back would be occupied by the captains of other tribes from neighbouring Provinces when additional forces were called up during a serious invasion threat.

All the evidence points to this. The many Testing Stones to test fitness; the numerous moot-hills which the small numbers of the local population never justified at any time; the large concentration of towers grouped on low ground further back: all these indicate the assembly ground of a large territorial army, with the twelve towers in Glen Lyon the launching points for directing troops up the hill passes to any point on the Pictish line. The pass names still recall their strategic use, for there is Fin Larig, Fion na Gleann, Coire an Fion etc. Indeed, there is also considerable evidence to prove that it was here, and not Scone, that was the capital of Pictland.

Radiating from Glen Lyon is a line of conventional hill forts that ran eastwards to Dunnottar, near Stonehaven, while another, more widely spaced, ran north-west to the Great Glen and beyond, and a third swings south-east to Stirling.

In the right foreground are the remains of one of the twelve 'Forts of Fionn' in Glen Lyon. Behind are the hill passes that give access to every point along the Pictish boundary. The Bhacain or Dog Stake can be seen at the bend in the road.

It is strange that there has been much speculation about the presence of small, broch-like, stone towers along these lines but little investigation of the core from which they sprang.

Imagine, then, a scene 1200 years ago when a Toiseach in one of the watch forts near Stirling first sights a new army of Angles advancing slowly across the marshy Carse of Stirling. Warning shouts are given, and the beacons blaze out from the summits above the old vitrified hill forts until a watcher in the tower on Ben Dorain spots them, and notes which line they come from. The runners are despatched — to the king in the glen below, and to the assembly grounds — and the warriors stop exercising with the Testing Stones, gather their weapons and assemble at their appointed moot-hills. Soon the whole army is moving purposefully towards Glen

Lyon, and marching through its narrow entrance to be directed to two or three of the towers which gave access to the passes in the direction of the invader. The troops split here, some to cross by the Pass of the Feinne to Fin Larig, while the remainder used other glens to reach Loch Tay, and perhaps were shipped to Ardtalnig. Somewhere the Angles would be trapped by this pincer movement and put to flight after a savage battle.

The towers and forts remained the main defence of Pictland until the death of Eaoghan, last of the Pictish kings, around 843 A.D. King Kenneth mac Alpin claimed the throne of all Scotland through his Pictish mother, and ensured a bloodless succession by inviting the six Maormers of Alba to a banquet at Scone where they were poisoned. There appears to have been no resistance by the now leaderless Feinne of the Province of Fortrenn, except that an ancient chronicle tells how the last of the Fingalian race in Glen Lyon was wiped out by the Picts at a battle near Coshieville. What the writer really should have written was that the remainder of the Feinne — the old palace guard of the Pictish kings — were destroyed by a Picto-Scot army of the new regime. Their burial mounds can still be seen by the banks of the Keltneyburn. However, it appears that the forts were still in use during King Kenneth's reign, for when a Viking raid swept right across Scotland it was halted at Cluny and Dunkeld, on the perimeter of the old military network.

Glen Lyon later became a favoured hunting ground of the Scottish kings. They erected wooden pavilions, and from these comes the name of the hamlet of Pubil, near Cashlie. When the chase had ended, the king and his nobles would feast and be entertained by the Bards who seem to have been rather numerous, for in the vicinity is a Bard's Pool, Bard's Field etc. These professional storytellers, although trained to pass down verbally genealogy and history, would be anxious to please their Picto-Scot patrons, so they would cleverly combine old Irish legends with Pictish history.

Now it can be seen how many of the Fingalian names in

the glen originated. Dargo's Castle should be Caisteal an Dearg — the Castle of the Red Man, i.e. Macbeth; The Castle of the Black (hero) is Macduff's Castle (in old chronicles 'MacDuff' is written as 'Niger', Latin for 'Black'). The Bhacain, or Dog Stake, was probably precisely this but to it would be tethered the hunting dogs of the kings of a united Scotland. To make the tales sound authentic in their new setting the Bards subtly altered local names and history, and thus the Feinne became the Fianna and the Pictish kings were amalgamated into Fionn, or Fingal. Possibly beneath Ossian's Grave in the Sma' Glen lay the son of a Pictish king, or could it have been an Angle called Oswin? The Bards are responsible for the obliteration of much ancient Pictish history.

In England at the same time, and for the same reasons, the minstrels were busy transforming the deeds of a native sixth-century cavalry commander into that of the armour-clad, chivalrous host of King Arthur and the Knights of the Round Table with which both Norman and Saxon could identify.

The spread of the Fingalian legends to over a thousand sites across Scotland is due to wandering Bards who, while the transposed stories were still in a state of flux, listened to local traditions attached to a tumulus, standing stone, or to some notable, and adapted it to fit in with one of the epic poems — to the gratification of their hosts who were providing food and shelter.

The Fingalian legend attached to Clan Campbell probably arose this way when some Bard, recalling that the heroic Diarmid ui Dubhne was the son of Fergus Cam Beul (Crooked Mouth), promptly associated this in poetic form with the new leader by marriage of the Clan O'Duine who had the same facial disfigurement. Space does not permit further examination of the rise of Clan Campbell, but its link with 'Diarmid's tomb' in Glenshee and elsewhere is also due to wandering Bards. There was, for instance, a king of Athol, Talorcan MacDrostain, who was lured to a hunting tryst by the High King Angus in 739 A.D. and drowned. Did he have an illicit relationship with the Ard-Righ's wife and thus become a local 'Diarmid'?

As the various local legends gradually consolidated into the standard form of the Ossianic epic poems, it can be seen how one Bard's 'Diarmid' in Glenshee, or Kintyre, became linked with another's celebrating a 'Diarmid' around Loch Aweside.

Thus over the centuries the real meaning of the 'Forts of Fionn' in the Glen Lyon area became forgotten as the Bards wove their stories around actual history and legend. Generations of Picto-Scots have listened enthralled to the stories of Fingal and the Fianna without knowing that their 'home' in Scotland was based on an extraordinary, and highly advanced, military defence system devised by a master race called Picts.

But man had lived in Glen Lyon long before the time of the Picts, for at the beginning of the glen are several well-preserved stone circles near the hamlet of Fortingall. This oddly English-looking hamlet seems rather out of place and was constructed in 1900 by the shipowner Sir Donald Currie.

The Oldest Tree in the World

In the churchyard here, supported by stone pillars, are the still growing remains of the famous yew tree — claimed to be the oldest piece of living vegetation in Europe. It is reckoned to have been here over three thousand years and it was a sapling when Nebuchadnezzar was King of Babylon, and an old tree when Christ was crucified, and an ancient giant when our recorded history began. In later times its wood was highly prized for arrow and tool making but the trunk gradually split due to fires being lit at its roots during the annual Beltane Rites, enacted here from pagan times until late last century. In 1769, when its girth was fifty-six feet, it was possible to drive a coach and horses through the middle. Since then the main stem has died, but new shoots have

The Bhacain, or Dog Stake, near Cashlie, in Glen Lyon. According to legend, here was tethered the mighty staghound Bran. More probably, it was used for the hunting dogs of the early Scottish kings.

become established to form a much reduced though still growing tree. Its branches overhang the burial place of the Stewarts of Garth, descendants of the notorious Alexander Stewart, third son of Robert II, better known as the 'Wolf of Badenoch'.

Was Pontius Pilate half Scots?

Fortingall's other claim to fame is the tradition that here was the birthplace of Pontius Pilate. Most modern guidebooks relate the story that his father was a Roman envoy who was visiting a local king in the hill fort of Dun Geal behind the village. However, the earthworks pointed out as a Roman camp are now known to be those of a medieval homestead.

The summit of Dun Geal contains only one of the sixth-century Pictish circular towers known as the White Fort; and it seems highly unlikely that the pregnant wife of a Roman officer would have accompanied her husband into what was then a remote and savage wilderness.

Yet this tradition of Pilate's birth is recorded in some of the early chronicles and seems so extraordinary a story to invent for this remote spot that there might just be some truth behind it. It is known, for instance, that after 10 B.C. Caesar Augustus sent peace envoys to many nations outwith the Roman Empire after a series of military defeats on the Continent had forced him to consolidate the empire and adopt a new policy of spreading the Pax Romana by persuasion and treaty. Thus when Cunobelinus became king of the powerful Trinobantes tribe of south-east England, Augustus sent envoys to him urging friendship with Rome, and the payment of tribute.

The Romans moved on to other tribes and, according to early chronicles, 'ane schort tyme eftir, the samyn ambassia-touris came to Metallanus, king of the Scottissmen', to bring him the emperor's greetings, and 'sundry goldin crownis and riche jewellis'. Metallanus, or Mainus, was not of course king of a united Scotland, but probably the elected, paramount leader of a Caledonian tribal confederacy. His seat was probably in the large, unrecorded earthwork camp the writer found on an eminence west of Balnacraig Farm at Fortingall, several hundred feet below the summit of Dun Geal.

Here the Roman envoys extolled the benefits of peace and friendship with Rome, pointing out that many southern tribes had entered into treaties, and had sent tribute to the emperor. The Romans had to wait many months for the king's reply, and for the snows to clear. They would, no doubt, have been given women by the king, for the Caledonian women were amoral and formed no permanent relationships.

Perhaps by the time Metallanus finally decided to send

'mony riche jewillis to be offerit to the August Emperor and his Romane Goddis', a companion of one of the envoys had given birth to a child. Both might have been taken back to the central Italian region of Samnium where they would have been given his father's family name of Pontii, one of the clans of the Samnites, and thus Pontius. Possibly his father educated his barbarian son, and when he grew up, made him a freed man, and gave him a Pilateus, the felt cap worn by a free slave.

Pontius Pilateus married Claudia Procula, the illegitimate grand-daughter of the Emperor Tiberius who succeeded to the throne in A.D. 14, and it was probably this marriage that ensured his promotion for he was given the rank of *equus*, or knight, and taken under the patronage of Lucius Sejanus, prefect of the Imperial Guard. Pontius Pilateus was appointed to the unimportant post of Governor of Judaea in A.D. 26, and it would not have been unusual for a freed slave to achieve this, for one such became Governor of Gaul.

Pilate's ten-year rule is described by the contemporary Jewish historians Philo and Josephus as cruel and unjust, and he is portrayed in the Gospels as being weak, but the length of his rule suggests he was neither incompetent nor inefficient.

However, he appears to have lacked imagination, for he misunderstood and scorned the volatile and deeply religious Jews, and his rule was marred by a succession of incidents. He allowed his troops to enter Jerusalem bearing standards with the image of their God-Emperor, and a riot ensued; he diverted Temple funds to build an aqueduct, and interfered with the adjacent autonomous princedom of Galilee ruled by Herod Antipas. Each time he was faced with a riot, or a possible protest to Rome, he backed down. Complaints about his rule began to reach Rome by A.D. 31, just as his patron Sejanus had been executed for treason, and Pilate became a worried man.

Two years later, the Sanhedrin, or Jewish Inner Council, brought before him a man called Jesus Christ whom they had found guilty of blasphemy under Jewish Law. Pilate was fascinated by this highly intelligent, enigmatic and dominating person, and could find no reason to execute Him. But the Sanhedrin were aware of the political pressure Pilate was under, and stated that if he released Him, he was obviously no friend of Caesar's. To save his political skin Pilate washed his hands of what must have seemed a fairly trivial incident at the time, and permitted the execution of Christ.

His rule continued till A.D. 36 when he made his final blunder by massacring a party of pilgrims in the belief that they were terrorists. He was recalled to Rome to answer charges of misrule. The Emperor Tiberius had died before he arrived, and he found himself without a friend at court. He was found guilty, and sent into exile, probably to Vienne in Gaul, and vanished from the pages of history.

But why was Fortingall remembered as his birthplace? The answer could be that Metallanus, following the example of many other tribal kings, sent either his son, or nephew, called Mansuteus, to be educated in Rome about A.D. 25. Here he later heard St. Peter preaching, and became converted to Christianity. Mansuteus would have been in Rome at the time of Pilate's trial, and would have learned then what happened to the child born in the Perthshire wilderness. According to tradition Mansuteus returned home about A.D. 52. Did he also bring back with him his disgraced and exiled kinsman to spend the rest of his days amongst his mother's people? Oddly enough, there was unearthed at Fortingall early this century a stone burial slab bearing the initials P.P. — but that, perhaps, is carrying things a bit too far!

Could it be that Pontius Pilate, remembered for all time as the executioner of Jesus Christ, was not only born, but also died, at the remote hamlet of Fortingall whose name means Fort of the Strangers?

But wherever the birthplace of Pontius Pilate, the religion of the Saviour he condemned to death came to these parts in the early seventh century when the famous missionary,

Adamnan, crossed over from Iona and climbed over the mountains into Glen Lyon to begin his missionary work. Here he became greatly loved by the local people who called him 'Eonan' and adopted him as the glen's patron saint.

Adamnan built his chapel, and a mill, at Milton Eonan near Bridge of Balgie, but just a few years later the dreaded Black Plague swept up the glen in 664 A.D. leaving not a soul alive. When it was only four miles from his church, Adamnan went to meet it. At a bend in the road, near Camusvrachan, stands the rocky hillock of Craig Fhionnaidh — one of the moot-hills of the Feinne — and up on top he climbed to pray while the people knelt below beseeching him for a miracle. After a while he descended, inserted his crucifix in a hole in a large stone, and ordered the Plague to enter — which it did! It probably helped that Adamnan had ordered all the healthy folk into the mountains while he remained behind to tend the sick.

Over thirteen hundred years have passed, but the saint's memory lingers still. A Bronze Age standing stone, with a crude cross carved upon it, marks the spot where the plague was halted, while beneath a bush across the road lies the stone with the hole into which the plague disappeared. Craig Fhiannaidh used to be a place of pilgrimage, and people climbed it to pray, and to see the saint's footstep imprinted in the stone.

After some years Adamnan left the area to return to Iona, and became famous as its abbot and as the biographer of St. Columba. In his old age he retired to the place where his early missionary work had been done, and when he died his body was carried down the glen in a hammock supported by bearing sticks inserted through willow rings, or 'duils'. When the first of these broke, the saint was buried at the spot, which henceforth became known as Dull. Thus says tradition, although more probably the name derives from the Gaelic word for a hillock. A church and school were erected, and the college later moved to Dunkeld, and then to St. Andrews to become Scotland's oldest university. The minister at Dull

Outside their lonely house of Tigh Nam Bodach, high up in the
mountains at the head of Glen Lyon, sit the Cailleach (Old Woman),
the Bodach (Old Man), and the smaller Nighean (the Daughter),
while two other children remain inside. This is probably the only
surviving shrine in Britain to the pagan Mother Goddess cult.
Photo: Dr Malcolm Murray.

still received part of his stipend from this famous seat of
learning until church revenues were re-organised earlier
this century. Adamnan's bell, one of only five still existing
from this period, can still be seen inside Fortingall church.

Unfortunately, Adamnan had been long dead when
another visitation of the plague occurred in the fourteenth
century. In a field opposite Fortingall is Carn na Marbh —
The Mound of the Dead — and a plaque on the stone pillar
on top records that the plague victims were brought here on
a sledge drawn by a white horse and led by an old woman.
They could not be buried in the churchyard for fear that

later interments would release the dreaded disease, and farmers over the centuries have steered their ploughs well clear.

After Adamnan had left the glen, and after the Feinne of the Pictish kings had been dispersed, the area was used as a hunting ground by successive monarchs of a united Scotland. In 1124 it had become known as the Glean Fasach — the Deserted Glen. So it remained until King Robert the Bruce granted it to William Oliphant, and its modern name first appears in a charter in 1328 where it is called Gleann Lithe — the Glen of Floods. However, there had never been a clan system, or a settled population, probably because it had been a restricted military area and the monarch's personal possession, and into the glen came settlers from elsewhere. The oldest recorded are the MacDiarmids, but also from Argyll came MacArthurs, MacCallums, MacGregors, Stewarts and Campbells. There were Menzies from Weem, Mac-Kerchars from Braemar, Robertsons and MacIvors from Rannoch, and later, after the '15 and '45 Uprisings, came MacDonalds from the north. These names comprised most of the population until around 1900.

William Oliphant's name mysteriously disappears, for King David Bruce gave the glen to his niece's husband, John MacDougall of Lorne. The new owner built his castle at Bridge of Balgie, then the hub of the glen, and the ruins of Tigh Iaian Duibh nan Lann — Black John of the Spear's House — can still be seen. Near it are the remains of the church he built at Kerrowmore in 1368 to save his wife's feet from the marshy ground around Adamnan's old chapel.

Black John of the Spears has passed into Highland legend not only as a 'king of lifting cattle' but also on account of the epic battle that occurred when the Clan Chisholm came to reclaim their stolen cows. The seven sons of Black John had been left to guard the castle, and were joined by one MacCallum the Cobbler. When the Chisholms attacked, the sons put up a valiant resistance, but six of them were killed, and the exultant Chisholm chief pushed up his visor to wipe his brow, before ordering the final attack. MacCallum the Cobbler seized his bow and fired, the arrow transfixed the hand of the chief to his head, and he toppled from his horse. Where he fell is still marked by a boulder called Clach an t'Sioslach — Chisholm's Stone — near Kerrowmore Farm, but it was split in two by a roadman last century.

In 1488 the most numerous clan in Glen Lyon were the MacIvors from Rannoch — until the day when their chief ordered the killing of Stewart of Garth's foster brother. This descendant of the famous Wolf of Badenoch vowed revenge, and asked to speak with the MacIvor chief on Craig Fhiannaidh.

As they met, the Stewart noticed something moving in the heather. 'What is that?' he asked suspiciously. 'Only a herd of roes frisking in the rocks,' came the too casual reply. 'Then it is time to call up my hounds,' cried the Stewart, and he waved his plaid round his head. His hidden clansmen sprang up from hiding, the MacIvors rose up to face them, and in the ensuing fight the MacIvors were badly beaten. They were pursued eight miles up the glen, where the remaining 150 were cut down. Their burial mounds can be seen at Camus Na Carn — the Field of the Cairns. Between Ruskich and Slatich is a large flat boulder called Leac nan Cuaran where the Stewarts left their sandals so that the number of their missing could be counted, and near Ruskich is the Laggan a Chath — the hollow where the first encounter took place. Thus the Stewarts acquired Glen Lyon, and were for a brief period its legal owners.

Shortly before this, a branch of the Clan MacGregor, driven from their ancestral lands in Glenstrae by the acquisitive Campbells of Glenorchy, had occupied the lands of Roro. Their most famous son was the noted Dean of Lismore, Sir James MacGregor, who produced the *Chronicle of Fortingall*, and made the first collection of Gaelic songs around 1512.

But the long tentacles of Clan Campbell began to stretch after them as Sir Duncan Campbell of Glenorchy began to acquire land by fair means and foul which others had held by right of the sword for centuries, and in 1502 Glen Lyon came into his ownership. He gave it to his son who built his house at Innerwick, and he was succeeded by Red Duncan the Hospitable who moved further down the glen to build a new castle called Dunan Glas in 1564. Its name was soon changed due to Red Duncan's hospitality, generous even by Highland standards, when he met a ragged bard on a hill path above the castle, and gave him all his clothing. Duncan's wife looked out from a window, and saw her husband quite naked on the hillside. 'Oh, such a large white goose!' she exclaimed, and from then on the castle became known as Carnban.

Kindly Duncan did not enjoy much luck in life. His chief, Grey Colin of Glenorchy, forced him to foster young Gregor MacGregor, heir to the chieftainship of Clan Gregor, and when the boy grew up he married Red Duncan's daughter. Then when he came of age he applied to Grey Colin to be invested with the ancestral lands of Glenstrae on Loch Awe which the Campbell chief held as landlord by dubious means. Grey Colin refused, and the insulted young Gregor gathered his now landless clan and embarked on a wild series of raids and killings on the Campbell estates.

In 1563 Grey Colin was 'legally' granted all the old MacGregor lands, and set out to exterminate the clan's troublesome young chief. The *Chronicle of Fortingall* records that year: 'Ane guid simmer, ane guid harist, except the laird of Glenorchy warreth against the MacGregors'. Gregor was hunted for seven years until in 1569 he was tracked by a band of Campbells with bloodhounds to Carnban Castle where he was visiting his wife. He made a daring escape, and was chased three miles down the glen to the narrowest point of the Pass of Lyon where he made an astonishing leap right across the river, and none dared follow.

An acrobat was killed last century when attempting the jump, and a mound by the roadside records his death — close to the five, tall larch trees that mark MacGregor's Leap.

To the left of Fortingall Church are the still growing remnants of the famous yew tree, reckoned to be over 3000 years old and the oldest piece of living vegetation in Europe. In the woods behind is a hill fort which might be the birthplace of Pontius Pilate.

Despite his incredible escape, Gregor was captured shortly afterwards, and after a summary trial at Finlarig, he was taken to Balloch (Taymouth Castle) and beheaded.

It is said his father-in-law signed the Deed that condemned him, and from that date the fateful destinies of Clan Gregor, the MacDonalds of Glencoe, and the Campbells of Glen Lyon became interwoven as all three moved steadily towards a common, final tragedy.

When Red Duncan died in 1578 his son Colin became laird, and shortly afterwards a band of caterans descended from Lochaber, and drove off sixty cattle. Colin appealed to the Privy Council but Edinburgh was a far cry from Glen Lyon, and nothing was done. Just after this he received a blow to the head that made him highly unpredictable, and gave him the name of Caillean Gorach — Mad Colin.

He had just moved from Carnban Castle in 1585 to a new tower house with a thatched roof, now the west wing of Meggernie Castle, when another party of caterans arrived and set fire to Carnban with lighted arrows, leaving it the ruin we see today. Colin captured thirty of them, and locked them in the cellar of Meggernie while he despatched his son to Edniburgh to demand justice. Before he returned Mad Colin received news that the Council seemed inclined to release the marauders. He promptly dragged them outside and shot the leader. When his son arrived home, he was greeted with the sight of the rest hanging from the trees along the avenue.

Fifty years later, Mad Colin's grandson died and left a widow who outlived three husbands at Meggernie. By her Campbell husband she had a son called Robert; by her second husband, Patrick Roy MacGregor, she had a daughter who became the grandmother of Rob Roy; while her third marriage to a Stewart of Appin resulted in a grand-daughter who married a son of MacDonald of Glencoe. Thus her son Robert was to execute the Massacre of Glencoe, while his niece had to flee for her life into a mountain blizzard to escape death at his hands.

But has history treated Robert Campbell of Glen Lyon unjustly? Certainly he was a hard-drinking wastrel who had borrowed heavily in previous years. His final act of folly was to convert Meggernie Castle into a stately home, despite being impoverished by several brutal raids on his lands by the Glencoe MacDonalds. He found himself ruined and his creditors began to press for payment, and soon the wooded slopes of the glen echoed to the crash of axes as the timber was sold. The charred roots are still visible all along the glen.

His tenants, even the MacGregors, offered him money, but as the Earl of Breadalbane had refused to lend him any more Robert vowed that no Campbell would ever again possess the glen, and in 1684 he sold the estate to the Earl of Tullibardine. He moved to his wife's property of Chesthill House, and the final blow came in 1689 when the Gallows Herd of the MacDonalds of Glencoe, returning from the Battle of Killiecrankie, stripped him of every cow, horse and piece of furniture he had left. He was now in abject poverty, with his family at starvation level. He joined the army and was stationed in Argyll, but it was at Chesthill that this sixty-year-old army captain received orders to proceed to Glencoe with his troops, and await instructions. No doubt the authorities had carefully selected him not only because it was the MacDonalds who had ruined him but also because he was in desperate need of the eight shillings a week pay.

In his defence, he had never engaged in any personal vendetta against the MacDonalds, and only one or two soldiers, like Duncan and John MacKerracher, actually came from Glen Lyon. The rest were Lowlanders and Campbells from elsewhere.

The troops were billeted in Glencoe over the winter of 1691—92, and it was while Robert was visiting his relative, and no doubt hearing his own cattle lowing in the byres, that he received his final orders — 'You are hereby ordered to fall upon the Rebells of Glencoe'. Robert became the scape-goat for the public outcry that followed, as no doubt had been planned, and he was promptly despatched to Flanders where he died in 1695.

Throughout the centuries the life of the common folk in Glen Lyon continued as it had always done, and the glen held a substantial and thriving population. There were large hamlets at Carnban, Bridge of Balgie, and Innerwick, while Invervar was a busy industrial village of which only the ruins of a circular lint mill can be seen. It was a hard existence for the crofters and often after the winter the cattle would be so weak from frequent bleedings to provide the family with black pudding that they had to be carried outside. The cattle would be gathered together ready for the great spring migrations to the lush grazings around the mountain sheilings, but before leaving, the ancient Beltane Rites were enacted. These date back long before Christian times, and were still carried out until late last century. Oatcakes, each with nine lumps, were roasted on a fire, and as each knob was broken off the herdsman tossed it over his shoulder with the words, 'This to thee, Oh Fox, spare my lambs; this to thee, Oh Crow . . .'

The Cailleach

But if the selected grazing ground was at the very head of the glen, then a very much more potent force had to be appeased — The Cailleach! No beast dared be moved until an advance party had gone up the glen, past Loch Lyon, and up Glen Cailleach to the lonely spot where the Old Woman has her house of Tigh nam Bodach. Fresh thatch was placed on the roof, the walls were repaired and then the stones known as the Old Woman and her Family were reverently brought outside to watch over the herds. Nothing but bad luck would come if she was displeased.

When the herds moved down in October, the family were carefully sealed up for the winter, and the house was made weathertight. This ritual was carried on for centuries until the pattern of farming changed, sheep replaced cattle, and the people of Glen Lyon were evicted or emigrated in their hundreds to the Lowlands and abroad. But the Cailleach is still there, as she has been since the mists of time. Her little house is now roofed with stones, and each successive generation of local shepherd or stalker looks after her and maintains the old tradition. Her present custodian is Bob Bissett, head stalker on the Invermeran estate. When I visited her lonely dwelling she was securely fastened in for the winter, along with her family of five.

The Cailleach and her Children are very heavy water-worn stones shaped like dumb-bells. The Cailleach herself is some eighteen inches high while her baby is only three —

though some people swear it is growing. Once every hundred years she bears another. This shrine is possibly connected with the pagan cult of the Mother Goddess, and may be the only surviving one in Britain. Strange and unpleasant things are supposed to happen if she is disturbed from her winter's sleep.

But there are other mysterious and supernatural things in this long and twisting glen. Beside the road in the Black Wood of Chesthill stood the tall upright Clach Tagnairn nan Cat — The Stone of the Devil Cat — and every Hallowe'en wildcats made a circle round it to welcome a huge, black cat that sat on top. A traveller who disturbed such a meeting in 1838 was savagely attacked. He managed to fight them off, and staggered torn and bleeding to Woodend House where a dead wildcat was found still clinging to his back. Opposite the Cat Stone was the Stone of the Demon, and it was here that one Macnab, Governor of Carnban Castle, broke his neck in a fall from his horse after being bewitched by the mother of a girl who had been forced to work naked in the fields.

Up near Cashlie in later times the Bhacain, or Dog Stake, was also used to protect maidens' virtue, for when the girls returned from harvesting in the godless Lowlands they were sent underneath it, and no unwanted children occurred. And near here is a flat moot-hill of the Feinne called Sithean Tom na Cloin — The Children's Fairy Hill — where, until the middle of last century, unbaptised children were buried at night for the fairies to take away.

The Haunting of Meggernie Castle

But the strangest story of the supernatural concerns Meggernie Castle.

After Robert Campbell was forced into bankruptcy in 1684 the Castle was sold to the Earl of Tullibardine who sold it in

The tower house to the left of Meggernie Castle was built in 1585 by Mad Colin Campbell — 3rd Laird of Glenlyon. It was extended to its present size in 1673 by Robert Campbell of Glenlyon, executioner of the infamous Massacre of Glencoe.

1689 to the family of Menzies of Culdares who held it until 1776.

One of the Menzies lairds is said to have murdered his wife in a jealous rage after falsely accusing her of infidelity. He cut her body in two and hid the parts inside a chest within a cupboard in the wall of the tower block. He then went off to the Continent, and when he returned a few months later, he said his wife had died abroad. On his first night home he removed the lower part of her body and buried it in the adjacent castle graveyard. He was returning for the upper part, but got no farther than the tower door where he was found dead in the morning. The circumstances suggested that someone had found out his guilty secret and murdered him.

In 1862, Meggernie was tenanted by an Englishman called Herbert Woods, who invited two friends, E. J. Simons and Beaumont Fetherstone, to join him for the stalking season. They arrived late at night after a long journey, and were allocated adjoining rooms in the old tower block. Simons was intrigued to find a sealed-off door in his room. He went to see Fetherstone, and together they examined the door which appeared to have communicated with both rooms, for there was also one in Fetherstone's room. Eventually they retired to bed.

At 2 a.m. Simons was wakened abruptly by what felt like a burning kiss on his cheek. He leapt from his bed, and was horrified to see the upper part of a woman's body drifting across the room and through the sealed-off door. Lighting his candle with trembling hands, he examined his face for burns, but could see none. He sat on his bed in great distress until his candle had burned out and daylight came.

When he heard Fetherstone stirring next door, he called, 'I've had a terrible night!' 'So have I,' came the reply. 'Look, don't tell me. Let's each go separately to Herbert (Woods) and see if our stories coincide.'

Their apologetic host later confirmed that both had had the same experience, though only Simons had received the kiss. The guests were subsequently allocated different rooms. Simons, however, seems to have been a receptive medium, for a few days later he was writing letters in the ground-floor drawing room when the door suddenly flew open. He went into the passageway, and was horrified to see the faint outline of a sad, beautiful face staring in at the window. Not surprisingly, he cut short his stay, and refused to visit Meggernie again. Unbeknown to him, many of the English servants had seen the same thing, and were threatening to leave.

Beaumont Fetherstone told his version of the incident in his diary: 'At Meggernie Castle, Perthshire, I was awakened at 2 a.m. by a purple light in the room, and saw a female at the foot of the bed. At first I took her for a housekeeper walking in her sleep. She came along the side of the bed and bent over me. I raised myself and she retreated and went into a small room made out of the thickness of the wall'. After following her across the room he was mystified by her sudden disappearance: 'The phantom seemed minus legs, which I am glad to say I didn't realise at the time or I should have been in a greater funk than I was'.

Meggernie was purchased in 1885 by the Lancashire millionaire John Bullough. During alteration work, the upper part of a skeleton was found beneath the floor inside the recess in the wall, and the bones were buried in the castle graveyard. However, this did not stop the manifestations. Dr. Norman MacKay, who practised at Aberfeldy for over forty years until retiring in 1948, used to relate an experience he had at Meggernie in 1928. He had been called out late to the Castle, and because of the patient's condition was obliged to stay the night. He was aware of the ghost legend, having been shown the haunted room on a previous visit, and was slightly surprised to find it was to be his bedroom. He lay on the bed fully dressed, in case of a sudden summons, and was awakened some hours later by a sound at the door. Assuming it was a servant, he sat up — only to see the upper part of a female body floating round the ceiling and gazing down at him!

I suppose a country doctor gets used to many things, for Dr. MacKay merely muttered, 'Good Lord! The Meggernie Ghost!' and then lay down to sleep again. In the morning he discovered that his bedroom was not, in fact, the haunted room, but the one below. He said later, 'Call it a vision if you like. Call it coincidence. If it was only a dream then it was by far the most vivid I have ever had'.

The interesting thing is that the haunted room had undergone alterations in the early 1920s. Where the ghost was floating about at ceiling level had originally been the floor of the room above.

Meggernie has been owned for most of this century by the tobacco family of Wills but in recent years has passed into other hands.

Today, Glen Lyon — this beautiful and mysterious glen of mountain and moor — lies empty, for the old population has gone, replaced by hydro-electric and forestry workers and those employed on the large sporting estates. Even tourists are rare, for the narrow, winding road ends abruptly at the modern hydro-electric dam that spans Loch Lyon at the head. Only the Stones of the Crooked Glen remain, mute testimony to 2000 years of recorded history, but the crofts and hamlets are in ruins, and now once again Glen Lyon is the Gleann Fasach — the Deserted Glen.

CHAPTER 3

The Curse of the Breadalbanes

Conquess and keepit things conquessit
> (*The Black Book of Taymouth*, circa 1590).

From Benmore to Kenmore,
The land is a' the Markiss's
> (From a poem in *Punch*, 1903).

In time the estates of Balloch will yield only one rent, then none at all, and the last laird will pass over Glenogle leaving nothing behind.
> (The Prophecies of the Lady of Lawers, circa 1680.)

Breadalbane — the heights of Alban — is the ancient name for the mountainous region between Ben More and Loch Tay. History, however, associates it with the mighty House of Campbell of Glenorchy and Breadalbane who, from a modest beginning, rose and rose with only one aim — to acquire land and more land regardless of all else. This they did with a savage intensity that far surpassed mere greed, and while greater nobles lost their heads and lands, the Campbells of Breadalbane emerged unscathed from the long centuries of strife. So successful were they that by 1920, almost 500 years after the family was founded, the then Marquis of Breadalbane possessed the greatest feudal land-holding ever known in Britain, totalling almost 500,000 acres. Yet, by 1948, a mere twenty-eight years later, all of it was gone as though it had never been.

The story of this remarkable family, who carved their name in Scotland's troubled history, began in 1432 when Sir Duncan Campbell of Lochawe, later 1st Lord Campbell and ancestor of the present Duke of Argyll, gave his younger son Colin the lands of Glenorchy and the island of Caol Chuirn (Kilchurn), at the head of Loch Awe, which had been forfeited earlier from the Clan McGregor. During Colin's seven-year absence on the Crusades, his wife, Janet Stewart of Lorn, used the estate rents to build a five-storey tower which forms the nucleus of the present castle of Kilchurn. On his return, Colin purchased the lands of Auchreoch, near Tyndrum, his first acquisition eastwards, and then in 1473 was granted the estate of Lawers on Loch Tay by James III. Next, he obtained the lands of Port of Tay at the east end of the loch with an adjacent island containing the ruins of a priory. This he converted into a castle, and made it his residence while acting as Baillie for the Crown lands of Discher and Toyer — the north and south shores of Loch Tay — a post which he held until his death in 1475.

His son Duncan purchased the lands of Finlarig with a castle, at Killin, and built a new castle on the island in Loch Tay. In 1513, he converted the many leases held locally into a new Barony of Finlarig, and by the time he died on Flodden Field later that year, he had acquired a large amount of land around Loch Tay. His son Colin succeeded him, and built a mausoleum beside the small castle of Finlarig 'to be ane burial for himself and his posteritie', as the *Black Book* has it, and within it, with only two exceptions this century, were buried all the lairds of Glenorchy and Breadalbane from that time on.

The rise of the Campbells of Glenorchy had so far been steady but uncontroversial — until Caillean Leath, Grey Colin, became 6th laird in 1550 at the age of 51. He was to rule for another thirty-three years, during which period he added substantially to the estates — and almost exterminated the Clan McGregor. Grey Colin now possessed all the ancestral lands of the McGregors, and had wardship of young Gregor McGregor, heir to the chieftainship. On coming of age in 1560, Gregor applied to Grey Colin to be invested in the clan lands, but this was refused. The entire Clan Gregor rose in revolt at this insult, and savagely raided Grey Colin's estates. Grey Colin was granted special powers to kill the McGregors, and used them ruthlessly, hunting down Gregor

McGregor for ten years until eventually capturing and beheading him at Balloch Castle in 1570.

Shortly after inheriting, Grey Colin had built a new castle at Balloch (now Taymouth) at the east end of Loch Tay. When asked why he had chosen this site when his lands at this point stretched no more than a quarter mile from the gates, he replied, 'Ou, we maun birze ayont!' He did indeed 'birze ayont' until his death in 1583 by converting many leases into secure feus through his influence with church and state. When he died, the *Chronicle of Fortingall* recorded, 'He was ane great justicar all his tyme though he sustenit the dedlie feud against the Clan Gregor — notwithstanding his tyrranny, his son and successor proved a still worse foe to us'. Those prophetic words ushered in the reign of the dread Black Duncan of the Cowl who was about 40 when he inherited and in the prime of his strength. He was grim, greedy and utterly ruthless. He acquired, by marriage, land in Menteith, Glendochart and Glenlochy, and by fair means or foul obtained land in Glen Falloch, Glen Lyon and Lorn. He acquired Achallader in Rannoch from the ancient family of Fletcher by directing his English groom to graze the horses in Fletcher's oatfield. The groom, unable to under-stand the chief's voluble Gaelic protests, merely smiled in reply. Whereupon the enraged Fletcher pulled up the iron tethering pin that secured the bridles, and hurled it at the servant, killing him instantly. Black Duncan emerged from hiding expressing regret, and said it was his painful duty to arrest him. However, as a favour to an old friend he would allow him to flee into exile, and suggested that the lands he made over to him on a temporary basis to avoid their forfeiture. The grateful Fletcher did so, shook his hand, and rushed off, and Black Duncan promptly registered the lands in his own name!

Through Black Duncan's many acquisitions, the whole area from Lorn in Argyll to Kenmore on Loch Tay began to piece together like a huge jigsaw. To protect his west flank he erected castles at Benderloch and Barcaldine; to protect

Beheading Pit with block and chains, Finlarig Castle, Killin.

the middle he improved Kilchurn and erected a castle at
Loch Dochart; and in the east he rebuilt Finlarig with an
adjacent beheading pit for any who opposed him. He
continued the persecution of the Clan McGregor who had
gone from one disaster to another until the fatal battle of
Glen Fruin in 1603 when they defeated the Colquhouns and
murdered some forty innocent bystanders.

The horrified King James VI and his Privy Council issued
new Letters of Fire and Sword against them and, backed with
the fullest authority, Black Duncan unleashed his fury. He
imported Italian bloodhounds, and is said to have had the
pups suckled by a McGregor woman to give them a taste for
her kinsfolk's flesh. He ruthlessly hunted down and killed
the McGregor men for bounty money, while their women
were branded on the face with a red hot key and sent as serfs
to the Borders, and the orphaned children left to starve.

Black Duncan was involved in plots of treason and murder
all his life. He attempted to poison his cousin, the Earl of

Argyll, he was implicated in the murder of the Bonnie Earl
of Moray and of Campbell of Calder, and yet, through his
friendship with the King, he escaped unscathed. Strangely
enough, he was also a landlord far ahead of his time for he
encouraged afforestation and agriculture, and enacted many
wise laws for the administration of his now vast estate.

He died at Balloch Castle in 1631, aged 78, with his name
both hated and feared. Those he had persecuted had their
revenge fourteen years later when Montrose's Highland
army, composed mainly of Macnabs, McGregors and
MacDonalds, descended upon Breadalbane in a savage whirlwind of rape, pillage and murder. Not a house was left
standing along Loch Tay, and the damage done from the
Ford of Lyon to the Point of Lismore was estimated at
£60,000.

Black Duncan's great-grandson, John Campbell, born in
1635, went to London at the age of 22 to seek his fortune, for
the family was now heavily in debt as a result of Montrose's
raid. After a lightning romance, he married Lady Mary
Rich, daughter of the Earl of Holland, and obtained with
her a dowry of £10,000. He returned home to Balloch, his
wife and he on one Highland pony, the gold on another,
while two ghillies trotted alongside, all the way from London.
Restless and ambitious, he obtained a commission to lead an
expedition against the Sinclairs of Caithness who had
invaded Sutherland, and while there met the aged Earl of
Caithness who was deeply in debt.

John Campbell advanced him more and more money until
the Earl owed him the sum of 1,000,000 merks, and it was
agreed between them that on the Earl's death John would
receive his title and estates in exchange for the loan. For
some extraordinary reason King Charles II agreed, and
when the Earl died in 1676, John Campbell was directed to
assume his title and the name of Sinclair. The rightful heir
protested loudly, and the king realised his error. He
annulled the previous patent, and in recompense created
John Campbell Earl of Brea d'Albyne and Holland, Viscount

Tay and Pentland, Lord Glenorchie, Benderloch, Ormelie, and Wick.

John Campbell, 1st Earl of Breadalbane, and 11th Laird of Glenorchy after his father's death in 1686, has a notorious place in history. Lord Macaulay wrote of him, 'He had learned the barbarian pride and savage ferocity of a Highland Chief, while in the Council Chambers of Edinburgh he contracted the taint of treachery and corruption'. A contemporary also described him as being 'as cunning as a fox, as wise as a serpent, but as slippery as an eel'.

He had adroitly switched his loyalty from James VII to William of Orange, and in 1690 proposed a scheme to pacify the Highlands by distributing the sum of £20,000 amongst the West Highland Clan Chiefs whom he summoned to a meeting at Achallader. The suspicious chiefs could not trust a man who supported two kings, and the meeting broke up without agreement, and with bitter words between the Earl and MacIan MacDonald of Glencoe, about some stolen cattle.

Thus were sown the seeds for the infamous Massacre of Glencoe, and when news of it reached London in February, 1691, John Campbell learned he was being held partly responsible. This he strongly denied — 'It's villanie to accuse me for Glenlyon's madness,' he wrote. Yet a kinsman of his had detained MacIan of Glencoe at Barcaldine Castle while he was on his way to swear allegiance; another kinsman, Campbell of Aberucehill, a Lord of Session, had a leading role in the decision to erase MacIan's late oath from the list presented to the Privy Council; and finally, his tragic 'cousine Robine' Campbell of Glenlyon had executed the massacre.

In addition, some £12,000 had not been distributed to the chiefs, but had disappeared, and when asked where it was, John Campbell had replied with the classic phrase, 'The money is spent, the Highlands are quiet, and that is the only way of accounting amongst friends'. His name was loathed throughout the Highlands, and yet at heart he remained a Jacobite for he sent his followers to fight at the Battle of

Sherifmuir in 1715, and achieved some popularity at last. He died at Balloch in 1717 aged 83, his huge estates crippled with debt as a result of his political intrigues.

His death marked the end of the turbulent centuries of Scottish history. The old clan system and tribal warfare were almost gone for good, as were the days of savage land acquisitions. Over the previous 400 years, the small family of Campbells of Glenorchy had risen remarkably without a natural clan following. John Campbell's son and grandson, the 2nd and 3rd Earls, began to improve the estates now that the area was settled. They introduced flax growing, and established lint mills and spinning schools all over the estates. Lead mines were opened at Tyndrum in 1739, and slowly the area became prosperous. The 3rd Earl laid out the present village of Kenmore in 1760 and let the houses rent-free to tradesmen. He died without an heir in 1782, and the Earldom passed to John Campbell of the cadet House of Carwhin.

The new 4th Earl continued to improve the estates, and abolished the old, inefficient run-rig method of farming. He introduced potatoes and turnips which solved the problem of winter feeding, cleared and drained the land, and granted long leases. He sent his tenants' sons to England to study modern farming methods, and by 1793 the population of Kenmore and Killin parishes numbered over 5,000 people, with 4,000 cattle and 42,000 sheep upon the hills. It was a bustling, prosperous area noted for its yarn manufacture, and its produce, and the value of the estates was enormous.

In 1799 the 4th Earl demolished the old castle of Balloch, and on its site built the huge Gothic mansion of Taymouth Castle which was finished by 1807. The cost was astronomical, for no expense was spared on the interior decorations which rank as some of the finest examples of Gothic Revival art in Britain. It was indeed a suitable residence for the owner of a huge and profitable estate. In 1831, the 4th Earl was created 1st Marquis of Breadalbane at the coronation of William IV, and when he died in 1834, he was greatly mourned throughout his lands.

His son, John Campbell, became 2nd Marquis at the age of 38 and was inordinately proud of his exalted position. Like many another landowner of that period, he followed the advice of the fashionable 'improvers', and before 1840 had evicted over 500 families from his estates and replaced them with sheep. He entertained Queen Victoria in lavish style at Taymouth in 1842 during her Highland tour, and it was then that the House of Glenorchy and Breadalbane reached its highest peak. However, with no security of tenure, more and more people drifted from the land and the infrastructure disintegrated. The 2nd Marquis died an unmourned and lonely death at Lausanne in 1862 whence his body was brought back to Finlarig for burial.

He had no children, and several claimants came forward to claim the title. This resulted in the famous Breadalbane Case which was not decided by the Court of Session until 1867 when John Gavin Campbell of Glenfalloch was declared the rightful heir. His son, Gavin Campbell, was created 3rd Marquis of Breadalbane in 1885, and held many offices of state and church, and directorships of many of the Scottish railway companies. He was a considerate landlord, but the first cracks were appearing for the sheep economy had failed, and now there were few left to pay rent. However, in 1900, the 3rd Marquis was the largest landowner in Britain with an estate of almost 500,000 acres which stretched unbroken right across Perthshire and Argyll, from Kenmore to the Atlantic. It was said he could ride a hundred miles east and west, and fifty north and south without leaving his lands.

The Marchioness, Alma Graham, daughter of the Duke of Montrose, was noted for her extravagances and her autocratic nature. As an example of the first, she once gambled £60,000 on a 'racing certainty' that remained in the paddock, and on another she cleared the grounds of Taymouth during an open day because some visitor had dared to address her without being spoken to first.

The Great War brought increased taxation, and its end brought depression, forcing the Marquis to sell 57,000 acres

John Campbell (1635–1717), 10th Laird of Glenorchy, created 1st Earl of Breadalbane in 1681. He purchased the estate of Lawers in 1693. The Lady of Lawers said of him: 'John of the three Johns, the worst that has come, or will come'; while a contemporary described him as being 'as cunning as a fox, as wise as a serpent, and as slippery as an eel'. He has a notorious place in history for his supposed complicity in the Massacre of Glencoe. Photo: Scottish National Portrait Gallery.

around Aberfeldy, Kenmore and Amulree in 1920. By 1922, he found it impossible to staff and maintain Taymouth, and sold it for conversion into a short-lived hotel venture to the Taymouth Castle Hotel company who still own it. The castle and 400 acres surrounding it were sold for £44,000 compared to a pre-war valuation of £377,000, while the sale of the family's seventeenth-century state coach raised only the paltry sum of £11. The Marquis moved to Craig Lodge,

Dalmally, and took ill while travelling from there to a board meeting in Glasgow, and died in the Central Hotel in October, 1922, aged 71.

As he had no children, he had directed that the estates be put in trust until the death of the Marchioness, who moved to Ardmaddy Castle, Nether Lorn, where she died in 1932. On her husband's instructions neither was buried in the mausoleum at Finlarig, but outside, in the courtyard, where their neglected graves now lie amongst the tumbled undergrowth and fallen masonry.

Before the Marchioness's death the trustees were forced to sell off Roro and Lochs in Glen Lyon, Edinample and Lochearnhead, Ardmaddy and Nether Lorn, the islands of Luing, Seil, Easdale, the Black Mount, Rannoch, Glen Etive and Glenfalloch in order to meet death duties and other taxes.

The Earldom passed in 1923 to Charles William Campbell, of the cadet House of Boreland of Glenlochy, who had followed a military career and spent most of his life in England. He was decorated in the Great War, and held many public offices and was a noted scholar. He entered into full possession of the estates in 1935 and made his main residence the mansion of Auchmore, Killin. However, the very depressed state of agriculture in the thirties forced many tenants to leave their farms, and it was necessary for the estate to purchase the outgoing farmer's stock of sheep at the theoretical value of 30/− a head, and resell them to the incoming tenant at the market value of 2/6d.

New regulations required large sums to be spent on modernising farmhouses, and fencing, and the estate was involved in heavy losses for rents were very low. In 1937, the estates of Ardeonaig and Auchlyne had to be sold, followed by Tyndrum in 1941, Glen Lochy in 1942, Glen Ogle in 1943, and most of the remaining lands. In 1940, the 9th Earl moved to Kinnell House, Killin, and both Auchmore and Taymouth became hospitals for Polish troops.

By 1946, all that was left of the once vast estates was

Kinnell House and a farm at Killin. Even the family mausoleum at Finlarig had crumbled into ruin. In 1948, the 9th Earl sold Kinnell House to Archibald Corrie Macnab, 22nd Chief of Macnab, who thus re-purchased his family's ancestral home and lands which the 1st Marquis of Breadalbane had bought from the bankrupt 17th Macnab chief in 1828. Nothing else was left, and the last laird of Breadalbane quit the area to make his residence at Invereil House at Dirleton East Lothian, until his death in 1959.

Auchmore became headquarters for the Hydro-Electric Board during the construction of the huge Breadalbane scheme and is now demolished. Taymouth became a Civil Defence Centre, then a school for American children in Europe and now lies empty. All that remain in the family are the ruined castles of Finlarig and Kilchurn on Loch Awe, which was the original springboard from which the family 'birzed ayont'.

The present 10th Earl of Breadalbane and Holland is John Romer Boreland Campbell, born 1919, who is also 20th chief of Glenorchy, Viscount Tay and Pentland, Lord Glenorchy, Benderloch, Ormelie and Wick, 14th Baronet of Glenorchy and Nova Scotia. As MacChailean mhic Dhonnachaidh he is second only to the Duke of Argyll as Chief of all the Campbells. He was wounded in the last war while serving as an officer in the Black Watch and was invalided home.

In 1946 he had a disagreement with his father and left home for good, never seeing him again. For the following thirteen years he worked at a variety of jobs including playing the bagpipes in the Golders Green Hippodrome, London, and when he succeeded to the title in 1959 he was working as a laboratory cleaner in that city, and known to his fellow workers simply as Jock Campbell. He lived until recently in a Hampstead flat, and believes he may be the last Earl of Breadalbane for he is unmarried, and knows of no other branch with a strong enough claim.

The lack of heirs was a principal cause of the downfall of the estate, and is known in the Highlands as the Curse of the

Breadalbanes. It took the Campbells of Glenorchy 500 years
to create the greatest landholding ever known in Britain,
and in a mere twenty-eight years all of it was gone. Perhaps
now the Curse has finally run its course.

Two Sides to a Song

IN BRAID ALBYN
LINES FROM BEN LAWERS
(To be read Scotto Voce)

From Kenmore
To Ben Mohr
The land is a' the Markiss's;
The mossy howes,
The heathery knowes,
An' ilka bonnie park is his.

The bearded goats,
The toozie stots,
An' a' the braxy carcases;
Ilk crofter's rent,
Ilk tinkler's tent,
An' ilka collie's bark is his.

The muir-cock's craw,
The piper's blaw,
The gillie's hard day's wark is his;
From Kenmore
To Ben Mohr
The Warld is a' the Markiss's!

When this famous poem was first published in *Punch* in
February, 1903, it was taken to be a humorous comment on
Gavin Campbell, 3rd Marquis of Breadalbane, who owned at
that time a vast landholding stretching unbroken from Loch
Tay to the Atlantic. A considerate landlord, the Marquis was
largely responsible for the building of the West Highland
Railway, and held high office in both Church and State. His

seat was Taymouth Castle at Kenmore, and certainly, in the halcyon days of the early 1900s, 'The Warld' was indeed 'a' the Markiss's!'

Since then, the poem has appeared many times in books on Perthshire, but a curious mystery surrounded its author. *Fair Perthshire*, published in 1930, states the poet to be James MacTavish, a farmer from Doune. Seven years later, an anthology of Scottish verse called *Oor Mither Tongue* also gave acknowledgment for the poem's reproduction to 'the proprietors of *Punch* and the trustees of the late James MacTavish'. However, that superb guide to the Lochtayside area, *In Famed Breadalbane*, first published in 1938 and recently reprinted, gives the author as one J. L. Robertson. This name was mentioned by the modern Scots poet Sydney Goodsir Smith in 1964 when he parodied the poem in his rollicking, Joycean book, *Carotid Cornucopius*, and called its author 'Jawbone Leakie Rabbitson'. Even today, books on Perthshire attribute the poem to either J. L. Robertson or James MacTavish.

I had assumed that the former must have been James Logie Robertson, a well-known poet of the period. Born at Milnathort in 1846, he was an Edinburgh schoolteacher who, under the pen name Hugh Haliburton, wrote many books of verse under such titles as *Ochil Idylls* and *Horace in Homespun*. His poems in the Doric were immensely popular, and during the First World War were pinned up on factory walls, at home and in the trenches of France.

James MacTavish, on the other hand, farmed near Doune in Perthshire, where his family had been for several generations. He was noted for the Blackface sheep he reared on the slopes of Uamh Mhor, but as far as I know he never wrote a line of poetry in his life.

To try to resolve this curious duplicity of authors, I wrote to *Punch* who unearthed their ledgers for 1903 and replied that, according to their records, payment for the poem had been made to one J. L. Robertson. This seemed pretty conclusive, and I reckoned that if James Logie Robertson

Taymouth Castle at Kenmore was built between 1801 and 1807 by the 1st Marquis of Breadalbane on the site of the old castle of Balloch. It is one of the finest examples of Gothic Revival architecture in Britain. The wing to the left was built for the visit of Queen Victoria in 1842. Including the surrounding parkland, the castle was valued in 1910 at £377,000 but reached only £44,000 when sold by the 3rd Marquis in 1922 to the Taymouth Castle Hotel Company who still own it. During the Second World War it was a military hospital, later a Civil Defence Training Centre, and is now empty.

did indeed write this famous poem, then it would certainly appear in one of his volumes of collected verse. However, despite an intensive search of all his published works, I could find no trace of 'In Braid Albyn', nor anything that resembled it.

I was prepared to leave the matter there when, by an almost unbelievable coincidence, I happened to be clearing out some old newspapers, and sheer luck made me read a 1942 issue of *The Scotsman*. In it I came upon a paragraph about the authorship of the poem which stated that James Logie Robertson had a brother called John who was an Edinburgh lawyer, and that it was he who had written the poem while on holiday at Loch Tay. The theme was suggested to him when a native of the area waved his hand at the mountains and exclaimed, 'It's a' the Markiss's'.

All the same, something didn't sound quite right. Why did so many books insist the author to be James MacTavish, the hill farmer from Doune who didn't write poetry? The matter might have remained a mystery but for Tom Weir.

I was taking part in one of Tom's *Weir's Way* television programmes featuring the Breadalbane area, and we discussed the poem while filming at Killin. Tom wanted to recite it while photographing the district from a helicopter, and, as these things happen, up from my subconscious came a recollection that somebody, somewhere, had related to me another verse which ended,

> Breadalbane's land the fair, the grand,
> Will no' be aye the Marquis's.

'That's great,' said Tom, 'I'd like to use that. Any chance of digging it out?'

That was the impetus I needed to begin a search which had a most surprising conclusion, for it finished far from the shores of Scotland. I decided first of all to track down the mysterious farmer, James MacTavish, and while researching in the Doune area, I stumbled upon an unpublished but privately circulated paper on local history. To my astonishment I found in this the complete and original poem of 'In Braid Albyn'. To my further surprise I discovered that the three verses which appeared in *Punch* were in fact the first part of a much longer poem, not written by either J. L. Robertson or James MacTavish; nor was it composed in 1903, but more than sixty years before, in 1840; and lastly, far from being a humorous comment on the 3rd Marquis of Breadalbane, it was written as a most savage and bitter attack on John Campbell, the 2nd Marquis, for his eviction policies between 1834 and 1850.

It seems that the original poem was written by James Kennedy, an evicted crofter and blacksmith from Lochtayside who had settled in Doune. His manuscript came into the possession of James MacTavish who was so fond of quoting from it that he was assumed to be its author.

The original would have been written in Gaelic, and was probably translated later. I can only assume that John Logie Robertson came upon the verses and adapted the first part into the then popular Scots for submission to *Punch*. It seems likely that his version became the accepted one, for in the poem I found that the style of the first verse is quite different from the rest.

Here then is what I believe is the complete and original poem under the title 'The Highland Crofter':

Frae Kenmore tae Ben More
The land is a' the Marquis's;
The mossy howes, the heathery knowes
An' ilka bonnie park is his;
The bearded goats, the towsie stots,
An' a' the braxie carcases;
Ilk crofter's rent, ilk tinkler's tent,
An ilka collie's bark is his;
The muir-cock's craw, the piper's blaw,
The ghillie's hard day's wark is his;
Frae Kenmore tae Ben More
The warld is a' the Marquis's.

The fish that swim, the birds that skim,
The fir, the ash, the birk is his;
The castle ha' sae big an' braw,
Yon diamond crusted dirk is his;
The roofless hame, a burning shame,
The factor's dirty wark is his;
The poor folk vexed, the lawyer's text,
Yon smirking legal shark is his;

Frae Kenmore tae Ben More
The warld is a' the Marquis's.

But near, mair near, God's voice we hear —
The dawn as weel's the dark is his;
The poet's dream, the patriot's theme,
The fire that lights the mirk is His.
They clearly show God's mills are slow
But sure, the handiwork is His;
And in His grace our hope we place;
Fair Freedom's sheltering ark is His.
The men that toil should own the soil —
A note as clear's the lark's is this —
Breadalbane's land — the fair, the grand —
Will no' be aye the Marquis's.

The background to this bitter poem is well known. A land that had teemed with people became a wilderness inhabited only by sheep. The 1st Marquis had raised over 1500 men from his estates for the Napoleonic Wars, but when his son tried to raise a fencible regiment in 1850, only a hundred men could be found, and none of them volunteered, 'Put your red coats on the backs of the sheep that have replaced the men,' was the cry when the Marquis came to recruit. The empty glens of Perthshire and Argyll are dotted today with the tumbledown walls of crofts and villages — mute testament to this terrible period of social upheaval.

The people emigrated all over the world, the majority to fates unknown. Those from the Aberfeldy and Glen Quaich areas went mostly to Canada where they cleared a wilderness in Ontario, and called it Perth County. In 1936, Miss Mary MacLennan of Stratford, Ontario, published a book in which she recorded many of the individual stories from survivors of the evicted crofters who settled in this area. Their struggle in a savage, untamed wilderness makes harrowing reading.

The story of the Glen Quaich evictions was also immortalised by the writer Annie S. Swan in her famous novel *Sheila*, written while living in the glen.

In the town of Shakespeare in Perth County stands a memorial cairn unveiled in 1936 by Lord Tweedsmuir (the novelist John Buchan), then Governor General of Canada. The plaque reads, 'Where sleeps the brave pioneers to North Easthope, Perth County, Ontario, Canada, who came from Perthshire, Scotland, from 1832—33 and 1841—45, principally from Glenqueich, Annatfauld, Aberfeldy, Amulree and Kenmore, 300 in all who came to North Easthope'. In time, the descendants of the early settlers moved on as their fortunes improved, leaving behind many small towns named after places in Perthshire and Argyll.

John Campbell, 2nd Marquis of Breadalbane, died a lonely, unmourned death at Lausanne in 1862 and was succeeded by a distant kinsman.

From then on began the downfall of the vast Breadalbane estates. Ironically, the sheep that replaced the people were partly responsible, for animals reared by the descendants of those evicted were imported cheaply into Britain from New Zealand, Australia and Canada. Today, none of the half-million acre estate remains in the Breadalbane family, and 'The Castle ha' sae big and braw' — Taymouth Castle — lies empty.

Truly, as James Kennedy wrote 144 years ago, 'God's mills are slow but sure', for the descendants of the evicted people of Perthshire have prospered greatly in their new homeland of Canada, while 'Breadalbane's Land — the fair, the grand' — is no longer 'a' the Marquis's'.

The Lady of Lawers

Seers, or predictors of the future, are a phenomenon characteristic of the Scottish Highlands. Perhaps the most remarkable of them all was Baintighearna Labhuir, the Lady of Lawers, who lived in the second half of the seventeenth century. Unlike others, her sayings were unambiguous and precise and, apart from three, all her predictions have been

Lord Tweedsmuir (John Buchan), Governor General of Canada, unveils the memorial cairn erected in 1936 at Shakespeare, North Easthope township, Perth County, Ontario, to the pioneers from Perthshire who first settled in this remote part of south Ontario after being evicted from their homeland. The inscription reads: 'Where sleeps the brave pioneers to North Easthope, Perth County, Ontario, Canada, who came from Perthshire, Scotland, from 1832–33 and 1841–45, principally from Glenquaich, Annatfauld, Shian, Aberfeldy, Amulree, Kenmore. 300 in all who came to North Easthope'.

fulfilled to the letter — the last coming true as recently as 1948.

Her prophecies are said to have been recorded during her lifetime in a manuscript called the Red Book of Balloch, which was described as being shaped like a barrel and fastened with twelve iron hoops, although this may have been its container. It lay for many years in the charter room of Taymouth Castle, but is now missing. However, her predictions were also handed down orally in Gaelic, from one generation to the next, until they were set down in writing late last century.

Exactly who the Lady of Lawers was is unknown, but she is believed to have been a Stewart of Appin who came as a bride to the small estate of Lawers on the north shore of Loch Tay about 1650. On her long journey from the west coast she was escorted by a party of clansmen known as Na Chombaich, Na Campanachd (The Colquhouns, The Companions), some of whom stayed on in the area, and in the Kenmore Parish Records of 200 years ago reference is made to their district of origin as 'Appin of Stewart'. They were actually Colquhouns (Chombaich) who had fought so bravely at the battle of Inverlochy in 1645 that Stewart of Appin took them into his service and gave them land in Duror.

They were also called Na Campanachd, The Companions, because they accompanied the Stewart chief and his family everywhere as a personal bodyguard and were famed as the heaviest and biggest men on the western mainland.

The family into which she married was that of Campbell of Lawers, founded in 1475 when Sir Colin Campbell of Glenorchy left the 40 merkland of Lawers to his son John, born to his fourth wife, Margaret Stirling of Keir. At that time it was the only land owned in Perthshire by the Campbells of Glenorchy who were later to expand dramatically beyond their small glen and island castle of Kilchurn at the head of Loch Awe in Argyll.

The cadet branch of Lawers existed uneasily alongside their senior kinsfolk who had ruthlessly extended their power and influence into the Breadalbane area, and there was a strained relationship between the two families. Sir James Campbell, the sixth laird of Lawers, was plunged into debt as a result of the savage raid on Breadalbane by Montrose's Highland army in 1664, during which the old Castle of Lawers was destroyed. The family moved to Fordrew, near Comrie, which they renamed Lawers.

A small two-storied, thatched house was built at Lawers on Loch Tay for a younger brother of Sir James, and it was he

whom the Lady of Lawers came to marry about 1650. She and
her husband lived only as tenants, for the estate was held as
security for debt by two Stirling merchants, and in 1693 it
was purchased by John Campbell, 11th Laird of Glenorchy,
and newly created 1st Earl of Breadalbane.

Lawers at this time was an important terminal for the ferry
from Ardtalnaig on the south shore of Loch Tay where the
main road came over the hills from the Sma' Glen and
Crieff. The ruins of the little harbour town still stand in the
woods at the foot of Lawers Burn, and, apart from being
roofless, the houses and streets are so well preserved that one
can easily imagine bustling activity.

To serve the expanding population, a new church was
erected in 1669 beside the House of Lawers, and it was while
the Lady was watching it near completion that she uttered
the first of her prophecies. *The ridging stones will never be
placed on the roof*, she declared. *If they are, then all my words are
false.* The workmen laughed. 'We'll prove the Lady to be a
liar,' they said and unloaded on the shore the carved,
sandstone capping stones they had brought by barge from
Kenmore. That night a violent storm swept Loch Tay, and
the waves washed the stones into deep water from where
they could not be recovered. One or two can still be seen
today, buried in the shingle.

The Lady was now regarded with some awe, and different
materials were brought in to finish the roof.

Her next prediction concerned an ash tree which she is
said to have planted on the north side of the church, and
beneath which she is said to have been buried alongside her
faithful Stewart servant, An Combach Ruadh, The Red-
Haired Companion. Her words were: *The tree will grow, and
when it reaches the gable the church will be split asunder, and this
will also happen when the red cairn on Ben Lawers falls.*

The tree reached the gable in 1833, and in that year a
violent thunderstorm demolished the west loft of the church
which fell into the middle of the building, causing it to be
abandoned as a place of worship from that time on. A cairn

Lady of Lawers House.

of red stones had been built on Ben Lawers by prospecting miners many years before. This collapsed in 1843, the year of the Disruption of the Church of Scotland, when the congregation of Lawers joined the Free Church. Thus the Lady correctly predicted the splitting in two of both the physical and spiritual church.

The ash tree was the subject of two other prophecies, the first of which was, *When the ash tree reaches the ridge of the church the House of Balloch will be without an heir.* This was fulfilled in 1862 when the tree reached that height, and in the same year the 2nd Marquis of Breadalbane, 15th Laird of Glenorchy, died without an heir. His residence was the mansion of Taymouth Castle which his father had built between 1801 and 1807 on the site of the old Castle of Balloch at Kenmore.

The Lady's final prediction about the tree was that *Evil will come to him who harms it.* No one dared to touch it until John Campbell, tenant of Milton Farm, felled the tree with an axe in 1895. Shortly after, he was gored to death by his own

Highland bull, while the neighbour who had assisted him went mad and was removed to the district asylum. Even the young horse that had dragged away the trunk inexplicably fell down dead.

Many of the Lady's predictions concerned the economic conditions of the area in which she lived, and one was: *There will be a mill on every stream, and a plough in every field, and the two sides of Loch Tay will become a kail garden.* At the time she said this the district was in a state of abject poverty, for Montrose's Highland army had gone through Breadalbane in a savage whirlwind of rape, pillage and murder, and only one house was left standing along the whole length of Loch Tay.

It was not until the end of the Jacobite Uprising of 1745 that the district was restored to full prosperity, although the 2nd Earl of Breadalbane, who had inherited the estates in 1717, had introduced the growing of flax in 1739. His son, the 3rd Earl, succeeded in 1752, and established mills at Lawers, Remony, Killin, Finlarig, Morenish, Carwhin, Crannich, Fearnan, Taymouth, Acharn, Ardeonaig and Cloichran. The mill at Killin processed 954 stones of flax in 1770, and the mill at Lawers 460 stones, and in that year yarn to the value of £1600 was exported.

These lint mills were the first of their kind in the Highlands and were the invention of Ewan Campbell of Lawers who travelled the Highlands building others, and died in 1817 aged 112. Thus, just as the Lady had predicted, there was indeed a mill on every stream that flowed into Loch Tay.

The 4th Earl of Breadalbane inherited in 1782 and abolished the old inefficient Highland method of run-rig farming in which alternate ridges, or rigs, in the cultivated fields were worked by different tenants. He granted long leases, compensated for improvements, and sent his tenants' sons to England to study crop rotation. He introduced potatoes and turnips and by 1790 both sides of Loch Tay were being intensively cultivated by over 700 tenant farmers, and there was a plough in every field in the area which was now a bustling and prosperous community.

At that time it would have been difficult to understand another of the Lady's prophecies: *The land will first be sifted, then riddled of its people.* However, when the 2nd Marquis of Breadalbane succeeded to the estates in 1834 he followed the advice of the 'improvers' and promptly evicted fifty-five families from the west end of Loch Tay. By 1838 another sixty families had been removed from Glenquaich near Amulree. The evictions were ruthlessly carried out, and as soon as the people were outside, the thatch was stripped from the croft roofs and set alight. Thus the land was first riddled, and it was sifted in the following years when over 500 families were evicted. In Glenorchy, the ancestral glen of the Campbells of Glenorchy and Breadalbane, the population in 1831 was 1806, and ten years later it was reduced to 831. Today it numbers no more than half a dozen. In 1800, the north and south shores of Loch Tay had a population of nearly 3500, and today it is no more than 100.

One of the Lady's best known predictions was, *The jaw of the sheep will drive the plough from the ground*, and this came to pass when the walls between the farms were levelled and vast areas of cultivated ground given over to flocks of sheep imported from the Borders.

With no security of tenure, the people drifted to the cities and abroad, leaving their stone houses to fall into ruin. Many small farms were joined into one, and the Lady was right when she said, *The homesteads on Loch Tay will be so far apart that a cock will not hear its neighbour crow*, for that is the situation today.

The old Highland culture was suppressed in the early Victorian era, and thus came true another of her predictions, *The feather of the goose will drive the memory from man.* Gone were the old sennachies who handed down ancient lore verbatim from one generation to the next. Those that remained were taught to read and write 'The English', and with the use of the written word the need for man's memory declined.

Perhaps the most interesting of the predictions of the Lady of Lawers are those concerning the Campbells of Glenorchy. She was alive when John Campbell, 1st Earl of Breadalbane, earned his notorious place in history for his supposed part in the Massacre of Glencoe. He purchased the estate of Lawers in 1693, and about 1681 the Lady uttered a saying that has since become known as the Curse of the Breadalbanes — *The Earldom will not descend beyond a grandson in one line.* The 1st Earl's grandson died without an heir in 1782. The Earldom then passed out of the main line to John Campbell of Carwhin whose son became the 2nd Marquis of Breadalbane and died without an heir in 1862. Then, as the Lady predicted, *Great and perplexing doubts will arise as to an heir.*

'Who would believe such incredulous nonsense?' wrote a Victorian historian in 1850 when informed of this prophecy, and yet he probably lived to regret his scoffing, for several claimants came forward to challenge for the title. The celebrated lawsuit, known as the Breadalbane Case, dragged on for five years until 1867 when the Court of Session decided that John Campbell of the cadet branch of Glenfalloch was the rightful heir. His son became the 3rd Marquis, and he, too, died without an heir in 1922. The earldom then passed to John Campbell of another cadet branch, Boreland of Glenlochy, and on his death in 1959 it passed to his son, John Romer Boreland Campbell, 10th Earl of Breadalbane and 20th Chief of Glenorchy, who is the present holder of the title. He is unmarried, and it is probable that eventually the Earldom will become extinct, and the Curse of the Breadalbanes will have run its course.

When both the Lady and the 1st Earl were alive she addressed him in the following words, *John of the three Johns, the worst that has come, or will come, but nothing will be right until Duncan arrives.* The 1st Earl was the third John and certainly the worst that had come. His eldest son, Duncan, Lord Ormelie, eloped with a daughter of the Laird of Lawers, and was excluded from inheriting by means of a peculiar clause in the patent of the title which allowed his father to nominate who should succeed him. Thus his brother John became the 2nd Earl — some say because of Duncan's unsuitable marriage, but more likely because Duncan was a Jacobite while John was a Hanoverian, and the wily Earl hoped that the estates would thus avoid forfeiture for his part in the 1715 Jacobite Uprising. So Duncan did arrive, but did not succeed, and eventually nothing did go right.

The next prediction was that *The House of Glenorchy will attain its height of glory when a boulder is covered with trees.* Which rock this was is not known, but the House of Glenorchy and Breadalbane was at its highest peak when the 2nd Marquis lavishly entertained Queen Victoria and Prince Albert in 1842 during their Highland tour.

The Lady's final predictions would have seemed unbelievable at that time, and yet they have come true in recent years. She claimed, *In time the estates of Balloch which were put together in hides will be put asunder in lace.* The vast estates had been acquired in large chunks, or hides, by judicial marriage, or by fair means or foul. The process of disintegration began in 1922 when the 3rd Marquis was forced to sell off Taymouth Castle and 50,000 acres at Kenmore to meet tax demands. After his death in 1922 the estates were put in trust until 1933, and during this period almost half the estates in Argyll and Perthshire were sold off in small lots, or lace, as the Lady referred to them.

The 9th Earl entered into full possession of the estates in 1935, but because of the depressed state of agriculture he was obliged to part with more and more until by 1946 another of the Lady's predictions came true, *In time the estates of Balloch will yield only one rent, and then none at all.* By this time the great landholding was reduced to Kinnell House at Killin, and one farm, and in 1948 even this last remnant was sold to

The last unfulfilled prediction of the Lady of Lawers is 'The time will come when Ben Lawers will become so cold it will chill and waste the land around it for seven miles'.

Archibald Corrie Macnab, and there was no property left to pay rent.

The last prediction of the Lady of Lawers about the Breadalbane family was that *The last laird will pass over Glenogle with a grey pony leaving nothing behind*. One person who saw this come true was Mr. James Anderson, now living in retirement in Killin, who was employed in 1946 as a gardener at Kinnell House. Like most of the people of the district he was acquainted with the prophecies of the Lady of Lawers, but even so he was astounded when he saw the Countess of Breadalbane arriving back from Killin station one day in 1946 with a trap drawn by a small, grey pony. He recalls turning to a colleague, and exclaiming, 'The grey pony of the Lady of Lawers! This is the end!' And when Kinnell was sold two years later in 1948, the last laird, the 9th

Earl of Breadalbane, did go over Glenogle leaving nothing behind, and with him went the little grey pony which Jimmy Anderson accompanied on the train.

A saying of the Lady's might be relevant to these days of consumer spending. It was carved on a stone near the summit of Ben Lawers until removed by a collector of curiosities last century, and read, *Spend as you get, And get as you spend, Save, and for whom, remember death*!

By the 1930s only two prophecies remained unfulfilled. The first was that *A ship driven by smoke will sink in Loch Tay with great loss of life*. This kept many local people, including the last Marquis, from using the pleasure steamers that used to ply the loch. However, a Gaelic scholar has re-translated this as 'When a ship driven by smoke comes to an end on Loch Tay there will come a great loss of life'. It is a curious fact that the last steam-driven vessel was withdrawn from service on Loch Tay in September, 1939, when the Second World War began.

Only one prophecy now remains. It is the most alarming of all. The Lady predicted, *The time will come when Ben Lawers will become so cold that it will chill and waste the land around for seven miles*. This might sound highly unlikely but let no one scoff. Remember that all the other predictions of the Lady of Lawers were equally unlikely — and all of them came true in the end.

CHAPTER 4

In Balquhidder and the Trossachs

The World's Worst Author

Dundee may boast of William McGonagall but Perthshire claims to have produced the world's worst author. He was Angus McDiarmid, who was born about 1770, and died about 1820. He was a ground officer on the Earl of Breadalbane's Edinample estate around Lochearnhead and lived most of his life there in the House of Cateran. Angus, like most of the local population, could speak only Gaelic and had no formal education but for some peculiar reason persuaded himself he was destined to be a great scholar. He became a fervent admirer of the great Dr. Samuel Johnson, after hearing the minister translate some of his works, and assumed that Johnson's pompous, turgid style was the ultimate in literary expression. Angus decided he would write a book, which, by carrying the Doctor's style to the extreme, would make him respected throughout the land.

Night after night Angus toiled by the light of a candle. He laboriously wrote the sentences in Gaelic first, then translated them directly into English using the minister's dictionary. The manuscript took years to write. Finally it was complete, much to the relief of the local people who were quite exhausted watching Angus staggering around the country-side with hand clasped to his forehead as he sought inspiration. It was probably for this reason that so many joined with local landowners to have the book published by subscription in 1815.

Angus decided on a simple title for his masterpiece: 'A Striking and Picturesque Delineation of the Grand, Beautiful, Wonderful and Interesting Scenery around Loch Earn'. The contents were quite remarkable. Here is a very small portion of a single sentence in which he describes a waterfall near Lochearnhead: 'Its force increases so potently that these divisions almost indiscriminate at which its incremental exorbitance transcended various objects of inquisitive per-adventure in such eminently measure that its homogenously could not be recognised at their interim except existing an emblem up to the waves of the ocean in tempestuous season. . . . . etc. etc.' What he meant was that several streams came together with some force and tumbled over rocks.

Angus Diarmid did not really deserve such mockery, for buried in the verbiage is a wealth of interest. He was the very first person to describe a crannog or lake dwelling, and correctly suggest its use long before it was generally known such a thing existed. He also describes a remarkable earthquake rift in the hills above Strathyre long before it was recorded by geologists. Perhaps if poor Angus had had a better education, the world might have praised him as the best of authors rather than the worst.

The Goldmine in Strathyre

Just along the hill from Angus's earthquake fault, and directly above old Balquhidder station, was sited a goldmine last century. The workings were of some size judging by the first Ordnance Survey map of this area, but are now covered by the uniform dark green firs that march over the hillside. The mine was established here about 1855 by John Campbell, 2nd Marquis of Breadalbane. He was an enthusiastic amateur geologist who became convinced the mountains of his vast estates contained a fortune in minerals. German experts were employed to comb the hills and in 1840 one of them discovered copper veins at Tomnadashan on the south shores of Loch Tay. These also contained deposits of silver and gold. Over the next thirteen years the Marquis poured thousands of pounds into this mine which produced a total of only 71 tons of saleable ore. Next came a sulphuric acid

The farmhouse of Edenbellie near Balfron. A top storey was removed last century but otherwise it is the same building as when the MacGregors kidnapped Jean Key.

works which was equally unsuccessful due to the cost of importing coal into what was then still a roadless wilderness. At that time coal could be bought in South Wales for 25p per ton, in Perth at 75p per ton, but at Kenmore on Loch Tay it cost £1.50 a ton.

About 1855 the Marquis was informed that a good vein of gold and silver had been found in the hills above Strathyre, and he established a mine high up on the hill. Gold had been known here for centuries. The local people used to place sheepskins in stream beds and the heavier gold would sink and become entrapped in the fleece. This was the actuality behind the legend of Jason and the Golden Fleece. In Balquhidder, however, the amounts found were minute indeed, and even the modern workings of the Marquis did not produce any great results. There was certainly some gold produced here but again the costs of transport prevented its being commercially viable. The death of the second

Marquis brought all further prospecting and mineral workings to an end in Breadalbane, and the gold mine in Strathyre was abandoned. Ironically, at the time of writing there is news of the discovery of gold deposits of possible commercial worth in the area to the north, and perhaps if the Marquis had lived longer, this part of Perthshire might have become as renowned as the Californian gold fields.

The Sons of Rob Roy

Balquhidder is closely linked with the famous Highland freebooter, Rob Roy MacGregor. Monachyle Tuarach between Loch Doine and Loch Voil was his first farm here. His father obtained the tenancy for him from the Marquis of Atholl in 1691 when Rob reached the age of 21. But it was after moving to Inversnaid in 1706 with his wife and young son Coll that most of Rob Roy's problems began. His vendetta against the Duke of Montrose and his factor Graham of Killearn; the brutal assault on his wife; the burning of his house; his part in the Uprising of 1715: all are well told in books, and on television and film. Less well known is the tragic story of the sons of Rob Roy.

James Mhor, his eldest son, was a notorious desperado. He led a pack of lawless caterans who pillaged the countryside, and made his four brothers to join him. The three older brothers, Colin, Ronald and Duncan, were persuaded by their father to settle down in Balquhidder. Unfortunately, the youngest boy, Robin Oig, had fallen under the dangerous spell of his older brother James, and still followed the wild ways.

On Rob Roy's death in 1734 James Mhor assumed leadership of the MacGregors of Balquhidder. He persuaded Robin Oig to kill one John MacLaren who had obtained the tenancy of Wester Invernenty farm which the MacGregors regarded as theirs. They waited for the return of their father's long Spanish gun from repair in Doune, and then Robin calmly took it down the glen and shot MacLaren in the back as he ploughed the disputed fields.

James Mhor, long accustomed to doing as he pleased, had not appreciated that the days of clan warfare were long past and that Lowland justice could now penetrate the Highlands. Such an outcry was raised that James, Colin, Ronald and Robin were all summoned to the High Court of Edinburgh to stand trial for murder. One Callum the Leech was also charged with having examined the fatal wound with a cabbage stalk and not doing anything else because he claimed he did not know with what shot Maclaren had been wounded. Callum, needless to say, was a friend of James Mhor! Only James, Colin, and Ronald appeared. Witnesses did not speak well of them, testifying they had 'beasts not rightly come by and that might be speired after'. They were said to be 'bad men, common thieves and harbourers and resetters of thieves'. A cynical jury listened to their pleas of ignorance of the crime and bound them over to keep the peace for seven years on sureties of £200 each.

Robin Oig meanwhile had fled the country and was outlawed. A reward was offered for his capture, the notice describing him as 'a tall lad aged about twenty, thin, pale coloured, squint eyed, brown hair, pock pitted, ill legged, in-kneed and broad footed'. Nothing is known of Robin Oig's movements for the next nine years, but in 1745 he is known to have joined the Hanoverian army and fought at the bloody Battle of Fontenoy. He was captured by the French and exchanged in 1746. He then joined the Black Watch and spent the next few years on the south coast of England guarding against a French invasion.

He was discharged in 1748 and made his way home to Balquhidder where no action appears to have been taken against him. The following year he married the daughter of Graham of Drunkie, and took over a farm which soon failed. Every other venture he tried failed too and then his young wife died in 1750. He was in despair and burdened with debt when James Mhor reappeared in the glen. James had joined

D

the Jacobite army but had been severely wounded at the Battle of Prestonpans. He had recovered and been in command of Jacobite troops in the north, but he and the MacGregors arrived too late to fight at Culloden. He was attainted for high treason but for some strange reason had been given a pass of safe conduct by the Lord Justice Clerk. James suggested Robin's only hope of salvation was to marry an heiress. He knew of a young widow called Jean Key who lived at Edenbellie Farm, near Balfron, and insisted Robin should visit her and propose marriage.

Robin's objections were brushed aside, and he reluctantly set off south the following day. He stayed the night of 2nd December, 1750, with an acquaintance at Cardross in Menteith and told him the purpose of his journey. His friend was astonished. Jean Key was barely nineteen and recently widowed after just ten months' marriage to John Wright of Easter Glins. She now lived with her mother and uncle at Edenbellie Farm. Her estate was reckoned to be worth 20,000 Scots merks and had an annual income of 2000 merks. These were vast sums by Highland standards.

The following day Robin made his way to Edenbellie with his friend who went in advance to the farm to make a proposal of marriage on Robin's behalf. The reaction was mixed. Jean burst into tears while her mother and uncle laughed openly. Memories of Rob Roy MacGregor's cattle-lifting exploits were still vivid in the district and MacGregors were regarded as little better than rogues and thieves.

Robin was not surprised at the rebuff but was more worried about facing James Mhor's wrath. As anticipated, his elder brother raged with fury at the news — probably more from losing a source of income than from insulted honour. He gathered a band of his old caterans, forced Robin and Colin to accompany them, and set off south. The heavily armed party crossed the Carse of Stirling by secret causeways and emerged on the moor behind Edenbellie.

The Key family were sitting round the fire after supper when they heard the sound of horses. There was a thunder of blows on the door and it burst open. A bunch of wild-eyed Highlanders entered and dragged Jean from her hiding place in a cupboard and bundled her outside on to Robin's horse. She tried to escape by throwing herself off but was thrown over the saddle like a sack of potatoes by James Mhor who threatened her with death if she tried it again. The horses were forced to a gallop northwards and at the edge of the marshy carse the party split up, with the caterans heading back to Balquhidder. The MacGregor brothers and Jean made for Drymen and the change-house at Mains of Buchanan where they woke the innkeeper and his wife and demanded refreshment. This couple both knew Jean well, and testified later she sobbed that she wished she hadn't a groat in the world. While they ate, James Mhor despatched a letter to a friend in Glasgow asking him to bring a minister to Rowardennan on Loch Lomondside by Monday morning.

Robin was beginning to regret the whole business particularly as Jean continued to cry bitterly. As they neared the loch he timidly suggested to James they release her. James's response was to pull out his pistol and threaten to kill Robin if he mentioned that again. They reached the house of Gilbert MacAlpine of Blairvockie and stayed till Monday when a minister arrived. There are strong suspicions that he was an impostor arranged by James. The wedding ceremony went ahead and the MacAlpines stated later that Jean went through with this cheerfully enough. Jean's aunt, however who arrived that night, said she was drugged throughout the proceedings.

Later, Jean was taken to her room and, according to which testimony is to be believed, she either took off her clothes and handed them to MacAlpine's wife, or she was forcibly stripped by the men. Either way, she was put to bed with Robin Oig and woke beside him next morning, when she was taken up Loch Lomond in a boat to James Mhor's aunt's house in Glen Falloch and from there to his own house in Glenducket. While there, James Mhor learned that warrants had been issued for the MacGregors' arrest, and he moved

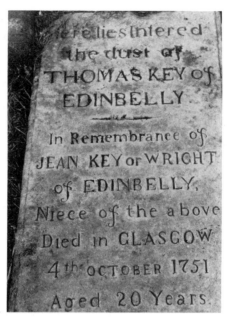

The gravestone commemorating Jean Key, in Kippen Old Churchyard.

the small party into the wintry wastes of North Perthshire where they avoided capture by moving rapidly around the hills. This must have been a fearful journey for a young girl brought up in relative comfort.

Her mother appealed to the Court of Session, asking them to appoint a judicial factor on her daughter's estate. This was granted and at the same time an organised party left Edinburgh to hunt down the kidnappers. James Mhor learned of this at Killin and threatened Jean with physical violence unless she appointed a friend of his instead as factor, but she had enough nerve left to refuse. The MacGregors and Jean now moved to Balquhidder where they stayed for several weeks. Robin and Jean attended the kirk together and were interviewed by the Session to ascertain whether they were truly man and wife. Three elders later testified that both answered freely in the affirmative.

It was beginning to dawn on James Mhor that his plans were coming apart but, confident now of Jean's acceptance of the situation, he decided they should all go to Edinburgh to present their case. First they called at the house in Cardross in Menteith of Robert Campbell, Sheriff Substitute of Perth, who told Jean he had the power to set her free. To his surprise she refused. The party went to Edinburgh where James engaged the services of the noted lawyer Henry Home who also testified later that Jean told him she was happily married. On the day of the hearing Jean disappeared and turned up that evening with a bizarre story of being kidnapped by a friend of the MacGregors who wanted her to leave Robin and marry him.

The Lords of Session, not surprisingly, found the whole affair too complex and interviewed Jean alone. She retracted all her previous statements and accused the MacGregors of forcibly marrying her to Robin Oig. Despite all this she still wanted to be his wife. The judges were suspicious of this new twist and directed her to be held in the custody of the court with only close relatives being allowed access. When her mother saw Jean for the first time after four months she did not recognise her and thought she had lost her mind.

At the next court hearing Jean said she did not wish to remain with Robin Oig and had only said this out of fear of James Mhor. This was obviously what the Lords of Session had suspected. She was freed and warrants were issued for the arrest of the MacGregors. James and Robin fled north into Lochaber where the former was captured in December, 1752, and brought south to Edinburgh. Jean Key returned home with her mother but, worn out by her trials, she died of smallpox five months later. She was buried in Kippen Churchyard where a simple stone records she died on October 4, 1751, aged twenty years. Robin remained in Lochaber, and it is my belief that he was the unknown assassin who shot Colin Campbell of Glenure in the Appin Murder for which an innocent man, James Stewart of the Glen, was hanged. The motive was revenge on the Stewarts of Appin who owned the disputed farm of Wester Invernenty in Balquhidder and who had leased it to the MacLarens instead of the MacGregors.

James Mhor stood trial on charges of hamesucken (armed housebreaking) and forcible abduction in July, 1752. The jury issued one of the oddest verdicts in Scottish legal history — he was found guilty on the first charge but not the second. Sentence was deferred for five months during which time James made a remarkable escape from Edinburgh Castle and fled to France where he died in abject poverty in Paris in September, 1754. Robin Oig was captured at a fair at Gartmore and stood trial in December, 1753. The jury brought in another strange verdict. He was found guilty of hamesucken and forcible abduction but not guilty of rape or forcible marriage. However, the first two charges carried the death penalty and he was sentenced to be hanged.

It is possible the jury may have reached the right verdict. Jean may have grown to like her kidnapper or perhaps become resigned to her fate. Such marriages had once been very common in the Highlands and were generally quite successful. Where the MacGregors went wrong was to try and emulate a way of life that was finished even before the death of their famous father.

Robin Oig was hanged in the Grassmarket in Edinburgh on 6th February, 1754. The *Caledonian Mercury* stated he was 'very genteely dressed . . . and behaved with great decency and declared he died an unworthy member of the Church of Rome'. His body was cut down and it is said that James Mhor's eldest daughter Catriona (the heroine of R. L. Stevenson's novel of the same name) seized the hangman's arm when he tried to take the dead man's clothes as his usual perquisite. 'You have already done enough and will not be allowed to touch any part of my uncle's dress', she is said to have cried out.

Robin's body was taken home to Balquhidder after being met at Linlithgow by a large body of the clan who didn't care to venture any nearer to Edinburgh and its legal authorities. He was interred in the same grave as his brother Coll who had died in 1735, alongside his mother and father outside the old kirk of Balquhidder. Perhaps Robin was guilty of terrible crimes but he appears to have been totally dominated by James Mhor. It is rather sad that the sons of Rob Roy should be remembered for such terrible deeds for, whatever their father's faults in the eye of the law, he was known even by his enemies as an honourable man.

The Minister of Fairyland

Another honourable man connected with Balquhidder is the Rev. Robert Kirk, minister here from 1664 to 1685. The bell he gifted the old, now ruinous, church can be seen inside the modern one. But it was not for his excellent ministry, nor his scholarly works, nor his gifts to Balquhidder church that Kirk is remembered today. It is because in the graveyard of the old church of Aberfoyle lies a tombstone engraved 'Rev Robert Kirk, 1644—1692', and yet it is common knowledge no body lies beneath, for the Reverend Robert Kirk was taken into Fairyland in the latter year and remains there still.

Robert Kirk was born in the manse of Aberfoyle in 1644, the seventh son of the Rev. James Kirk, the then minister. The family were desperately poor because his father's 'house, corn, books, and haill guids had been destroyed by the cruelty of the rebels'. He had exhausted his patrimony and wife's tocher of eleven merks trying to obtain legal redress against 'a strong party of cruel and barbarous Highlanders' who presumably were part of the Great Montrose's Highland army.

Despite their poverty, his father ensured Robert received a good education by sending him to the High School of

The Doon Hill lies behind Aberfoyle Old Churchyard. There is now a 'Fairy Trail' leading to the top.

Dundee. From there he went to Edinburgh University where he graduated with a Master of Arts degree in 1661. He was granted a bursary by the Presbytery of Dunblane to study theology at St. Andrews University where he was a brilliant scholar, being awarded the degree of Doctor of Divinity in 1664 at the age of 20. In the same year he was appointed minister of Balquhidder, and flung himself with zest into the heavy workload of his scattered parish.

From the sparse records available, he emerges as a compassionate man. When Bishop Ramsay at Dunblane 'did enquyre at Robert Kirk, minister of Balquhidder, what he had done anent Duncane Ferguson adulterer in that paroch, agines whom the sentence of excommunicacione was to be denounced', Kirk replied he had not yet put the punishment into effect as he was hopeful of bringing the man to repentence.

He also spent some of his own stipend on enhancing the church, and in 1684 ordered a new bell from Meikle of Edinburgh. It was engraved 'For Balquhidder Church:

Robert Kirke Minister: Love and Life; Anno 1684', and was in use until 1896 when it cracked. It was stolen from Balquhidder church in 1973, but later recovered from an Airdrie scrapyard, and now sits on an old oak chest within the present building.

Kirk also found time for scholarly work and translated the first hundred psalms into Gaelic. He was also commissioned to transcribe Bishop Bedell's Irish Bible into Scots Gaelic. This was a monumental task, for the Irish version used different characters which had to be laboriously transcribed into the Roman ones familiar to the Highlanders. He travelled to London in connection with the book's publication and maintained a neat journal of his travels. A copy of Kirk's Gaelic Bible is kept in a glass case in Balquhidder church.

In 1670, he married Isobel, daughter of Sir Colin Campbell of Mochaster, who bore him two children. Sadly, she died on Christmas Day, 1680, and the grief-stricken widower had a gravestone made for her which can still be seen in Balquhidder churchyard. Unfortunately, the sad verses he composed in her memory are now indecipherable.

He flung himself into even more church work, and in the next few years undertook tours of inspection in other parishes and various missions for the Synod of Dunblane. He also married again, this time a daughter of Campbell of Fordy. She bore him a son who later became minister at Dornoch.

Robert Kirk was appointed minister of Aberfoyle in 1685, and moved his family to the old manse near the small church in the Kirktoun of Aberfoyle. He was then 41, with a reputation of being an earnest, dedicated, and academic churchman, held in high regard by his superiors. However, he had been in his new charge only a short time when a strange change came over him. Behind the old manse lies the Doon Hill, reputed to be a *Dun Sithean*, or Fairy Hill, and to this place Robert Kirk became inextricably drawn. Night after night, he would go and lie on the hill with his ears pressed to the ground, and would leave reluctantly only when his anxious wife came in search of him.

Then, in 1690, this hitherto highly conventional and respectable minister began to write a strange and extra-ordinary manuscript. He called it 'The Secret Commonwealth of Elves, Fauns and Fairies', and it was nothing less than a detailed account of the Fairy People he had communicated with on the Doon Hill. He describes them as the *Siths, Sleagh Maith,* or *Doine Shi* — The People of Peace. These names can be found all over Scotland in such places as Glen Shee, Schiehallion, and Ben Shie, while the word *Banshee* has passed into the English language. All over the Highlands are hundreds of hills and mounds with names beginning *Sith* or *Sithean.*

Kirk stated that the Fairies he saw had 'Apparel and Speech like that of the people and Countrey under which they live; so are they seen to wear Plaids and variegated Garments in the Highlands of Scotland. They speak little, and that by way of whistling, clear, not rough . . . Their bodies be so plyable through the Subillity of the Spirits that agitate them, that they can make them appear or disappear at pleasure'.

He described in great detail the lives and habits of the Fairy People, all of it recorded in a perfectly matter-of-fact manner. Kirk also makes much mention of the gift of Second Sight which he appears to have had himself. Again, quite undramatically, he tells that someone who had the Sight in Balquhidder was nearly trapped in Fairyland, but managed to cut one of the Fairies with an iron knife. The Fairies, he says, 'are terryfyed by nothing so much as cold iron'. However, this incident was unusual because 'his neighbours often perceaved this Man to disapear at a certane place, and about an hour later to become visible, and to discover him selfe a Bow-Shot from the first place'.

He also tells how he and another clergyman examined a woman who had wandered off in search of sheep and had lain down to rest on a Fairy hillock. She found herself transported to another place before day and then returned later.

Perhaps Robert Kirk revealed too much about this strange

and secret world to which he alone was privy. What happened next was recorded by the Rev. Robert Graham, a later successor to the charge of Aberfoyle. It seems that in May 1692, shortly after he had completed his manuscript, Kirk left the manse one night, clad only in his nightgown. He was drawn to the Doon Hill, where he fell down in a fit, apparently dead. A funeral service was held, although it is said the coffin was filled with stones and that his body had disappeared.

A few days later, Robert Kirk appeared before a relative, and told him to speak to a local laird, Graham of Duchray, who was related to both, and inform him he was not dead. Kirk said he had fallen in a swoon and was carried into Fairyland, but would appear again on the birth of his child. When that time came, Graham of Duchray was to throw a knife over his head and he would then be returned to the living. Perhaps not surprisingly, the relative did not at first pass on his extraordinary message, but Robert Kirk materialised before him again, threatening to re-appear every night until he did so.

Graham of Duchray was eventually told, and in fairness did bring along a knife to the baptism at the manse. The house was crowded with guests and just as the service finished, the very solid form of Robert Kirk walked through the door. Alas, Graham of Duchray was so stunned he just sat and gaped. Kirk gave him a reproachful look before walking past and leaving by another door. He was never seen again and it is believed that he remains trapped in Fairyland to the present day.

Colin Kirk, the minister's eldest son and an Edinburgh lawyer, had no doubts about what had happened to his father. 'He has gone to his own kind', he wrote to a friend. His father's strange document passed to him and was lost for a time until rediscovered by Sir Walter Scott in 1815. It was printed in 1893, and again in 1933 by Aenas MacKay of Stirling. The original is now in Edinburgh University Library.

In 1908, W. Y. Evans Wentz, a renowned American recorder of Celtic fairy lore, visited the churchyard of Aberfoyle and wrote, in a long-winded sentence, 'Mrs. J. MacGregor, who keeps the key to the old churchyard, where there is a tomb to Kirk, though many say that there is nothing but a coffin filled with stones, told me that Kirk was taken into the Fairy Knoll, which she pointed to across a little valley in front of us, and is there yet, for the hill is full of caverns, and in them 'the Good People' have their homes'.

Some scholars see in this strange story several elements of Celtic folklore, although admittedly in an unusual form. However, they say the date is rather late for this type of story to evolve. Others see in Kirk's manuscript aspects of the mystical Rosicrucian cult which was beginning to flourish at that time and is now incorporated into the Scottish Rites of Freemasonry. Indeed, the first allusion to the Rosicrucians appeared in 1638 in the *Muses Threnodie* of Henry Adamson — 'For we are the Brethren of the Rosie Cross. We have the Mason's word and second sight' — and we know that Kirk was a mason. But much of what Kirk wrote has been recorded as happening to other people since, and similar instances of the Second Sight can be found in Elizabeth Sutherland's latest book *Ravens and Black Rain*, which details incidents to the present day. What makes Kirk's writings unique is his detailed account of Fairyland.

Of course, cynics will dismiss all this as nonsense. But is it? I have in front of me a newspaper cutting from the 1930s which tells how an Irish girl set out to climb the Fairy Hill of Lis Aird in County Mayo. She tried to come back down, but found herself trapped by an invisible barrier. She realised she was invisible herself when a search party passed and re-passed beside her but failed to hear her shouts. It was hours later before she suddenly found herself free, and materialised before the astounded searchers.

Then there is the case, in 1951, when a man dressed in the clothes of a bygone period suddenly materialised in the middle of a busy New York street. He stared in bewilderment

Jules Verne (1828–1905). His visit to Scotland in 1859 inspired him to write his classic novels, and in *Black Diamonds* he sited a fictional vast coalmine beneath The Trossachs.

at the oncoming traffic, tried to run, but was knocked down and killed by a car. The only clue to his identity was a receipt referring to a livery stable which had been in existence eighty years before.

Robert Kirk made much mention of people disappearing on Fairy Hills and being transported to another place. Extraordinarily similar is the incident described in the best-selling book by Charles Berlitz, *The Philadelphia Experiment*. According to this, a US naval warship, the *USS Eldridge*, was the subject of a top-secret trial in 1943 to prove Einstein's Unified Field Theory. Three hundred tons of electrical equipment was apparently put aboard and when it was switched on, a fog enveloped the ship. According to an eye witness, the vessel was suddenly transported a hundred miles from the dockyard at Philadelphia to Norfolk, Virginia. It remained there for a minute before re-appearing at its base. According to the book, the effect on the crew was disastrous. Several disappeared completely, some made appearances afterwards and then vanished again, while others went mad. Some survivors told of being trapped in a fog which rendered them invisible. Now, if that experiment took place — and it is still denied by the authorities — then it involved electro-magnetic radiation. A theory gaining ground suggests that stone circles and standing stones were sited in lines which followed faults in the earth's surface, where pressure on the rock below produced an enhanced electromagnetic field. It is interesting that the Fairy Hill of Aberfoyle lies on one of these ley lines. Is it possible that Robert Kirk, with his mind so receptive to the paranormal, became trapped in one such field? The 'fairies' he describes, and their clothes and weapons, have an uncanny similarity to the people of the Neolithic and Bronze Age period. Were these the 'fairies' he could see?

Would the iron knife flung over his head have short-circuited the field and let him step back out of the warp in the earth's magnetic field? It really isn't so strange, for there is no reason why the magnetic field of the earth should not act in exactly the same manner as a video recorder, for the principle is the same.

Today the Doon Hill at Aberfoyle is laid out with walks, and many visitors follow the 'Fairy Path' indicated by some incongruous signposts painted with toadstools. I often wonder what would happen if something caused the Rev. Robert Kirk to re-appear before a startled party of tourists — or what would happen if the self-same party disappeared into 'Fairyland'?

We are gradually realising that the earth holds many mysteries that science cannot fathom. Perhaps one day we, too, will understand the secrets of Robert Kirk's Fairyland.

Jules Verne and the Trossachs Coalmine

Sir Walter Scott can be credited with founding Scotland's tourist trade, and in making the Trossachs area renowned worldwide. One of his greatest fans was the French novelist Jules Verne, author of such classics as *Around the World in Eighty Days* and *Twenty Thousand Leagues Under the Sea*. However, I fancy Sir Walter would have turned in his grave if he had known Verne would site a coalmine — albeit a fictional one — at Aberfoyle.

Jules Verne was born in Brittany in 1828, the son of a Nantes lawyer who wanted him to study for the legal profession. His mother was descended from a fifteenth-century Scots archer who had remained in France after some war or other. Verne did study law for a time but abandoned it when he was 23. He began to write short stories and farces for the Paris stage and in 1857 married a young widow with two children. He started work as a stockbroker to support them but they were desperately poor. Verne rose each morning at five o'clock and wrote till ten when he left for the Bourse. He read avidly in every spare moment, particularly the works of Sir Walter Scott whom he fervently admired, and who inspired in him a great love of the romance of Scotland. Scott's blend of accurate, picturesque description and action in place of character analysis was the greatest influence on Verne's own writings.

When Verne was 31, the father of a friend offered the friend and Verne a free trip to Britain on one of the ships he managed. They arrived at Liverpool in July, 1859, and took the train north. Verne was so keen to see the Trossachs that rather prematurely he cried out 'At last! The land of Fergus McIvor', when sighting the hills of the Lake District.

They stayed in a Princes Street hotel and from there explored Edinburgh. Verne was appalled at the poverty he saw, and in his journal describes it vividly: 'Canongate is Edinburgh's street of shame — and it leads to the Royal

Castle! Naked children, barefoot women and children in rags, beggars holding out hats, all collide, pass, stumble, limp and sidle with famished faces beneath the tall house fronts. Surrounded by this poverty-stricken crowd, in this pestilential atmosphere, on the heavy, muddy cobblestones of the foul, dark, damp, little streets called "closes" that lead to vile slums stumbling down into the nearby ravines, one yet encounters the terrible poverty of old Scotland. The Canongate is incomparable; it is unique, sui generis. Its stalls and shops, its signboards creaking in their iron rings, its overhanging roofs, its prison clock looming in mid-street, its ancient hostelries — all this cries out for the brush of Delacroix'.

Later they boarded a steamer for Stirling but landed at Crombie Point in Fife due to a storm and there joined a train for Glasgow. On the way they passed the depressed coalfields and industry around Alloa and Stirling and Jules Verne gazed out of the window in raptures. His hero, Sir Walter Scott, may have been inspired by the scenery and ruined castles and abbeys, but Verne was the first writer to appreciate that abandoned, derelict machinery has a poetic beauty of its own. It was this unplanned train journey that was the basis for most of Verne's classic novels.

Jules and his friend stayed in Glasgow and from there took a trip up Loch Lomond to Inversnaid where they boarded a stagecoach which took them to the Trossachs for a sail on Loch Katrine. From here they travelled to Callander and back to Glasgow. Verne was delighted with the tour on which he eagerly searched out every scene from Scott's novels and made careful notes.

Later they would sail from the Clyde 'past the small hamlet of Partick' and, a short distance further on, 'in place of timber yards, covered wharfs, tall factories, gigantic iron scaffolding which looked like the cages of a menagerie, now appeared coquettish houses, cottages buried amongst trees and villas of Anglo Saxon design scattered over the green hills'. Their route took them past Rothesay and Arran to the

Crinan Canal where they disembarked into a smaller craft. 'While the canal men open the gates, young girls come politely and offer the passengers fresh milk, speaking with that Gaelic idiom very often incomprehensible to the English', recorded Verne.

The pair then toured the Hebrides with Verne again ecstatic about the scenery. Staffa really caught his imagination. 'What an enchanting place is this Fingal's Cave! Who could be so dull of soul as not to believe it was created by a God for the sylphs and water nymphs?' It is hardly surprising that he later set one of his novels inside the cave and that echoes of it can be found in several of his more famous novels, particularly *Journey to the Centre of the Earth* and *The Mysterious Island*.

Jules Verne wrote an account of his Scottish tour during the winter of 1859 as a slightly fictionalised story entitled *Voyage en Ecosse*, but his publisher thought it too light. His first novel, *Five Weeks in a Balloon*, appeared in 1863, the first of a remarkable output of sixty-five novels. His writings made him extremely rich and he paid a second visit to Scotland in 1879 in his private yacht.

Verne had a great affection for Scotland and the Scots. His fifth novel, *The Children of Captain Grant*, tells of an independent Scots colony in the South Seas, and Scotsmen are to be found in most of his novels.

In 1877 he wrote *Les Indes Noires* (*Black Diamonds*) which virtually traces Verne's travels from Edinburgh to the Trossachs. The characters travel by precisely the same route, see the same sights, stay at the same hotels and use the same steamers and trains. The novel is about the re-opening of an abandoned coalmine beneath Aberfoyle, and when a wall is blasted through, a vast cavern is revealed. This is found to stretch as far north as the Caledonian Canal, south to Dundonald Castle near Irvine, east to Alloa, and west to Dumbarton. An underground town is built beside a sub-terranean loch, and Verne, remembering the wretched state of the people of Edinburgh and Alloa, suggested that in future such a place might serve as a refuge for the working classes due to the equable climate. The geology and methods of coalmining are explained in great detail, for Verne's research was painstaking. Equally astonishing is the vast knowledge he acquired about Scotland and its history.

Jules Verne did not allow his admiration for Sir Walter Scott and the Trossachs to prevent his siting a fictional coalmine in this beautiful area. At the beginning of the book two of the characters are walking the four miles from Callander station to 'the Yarrow Shaft, Dochart Pit, Aberfoyle'. Verne describes their feelings thus: 'Agricultural life had now replaced the more active, noisy life of industry . . . James Starr might well have been traversing a desert . . . The engineer gazed about him with sadness . . . on the horizon none of these black vapours which the manufacturer loves to see, no tall cylindrical chimneys vomited out smoke . . . the ground, formerly blackened by coal dust, had a clean look'.

At the end of the book, after Loch Katrine has disappeared into the mine below, Verne writes, 'Sir Walter Scott would have died of despair'. I rather fancy Sir Walter would have collapsed many times after hearing his beloved Trossachs described in such a manner but this was what Verne's public wanted to read. The excitement of new discoveries, scientific advancement, and thrusting industry creating new wealth made the Victorians ignore the exploitation of man and nature. *Black Diamonds* is not one of Verne's better books and is almost unknown, but it does reveal the depth of Verne's knowledge of Scotland. I learned from reading it that Dumbarton Castle was the first choice for the imprisonment of Napoleon Bonaparte and that Cromwell's mother was a Stuart of Rosyth. It also gives an excellent description of west Perthshire in mid-Victorian times. Similarly, *Le Rayon Vert* (*The Green Ray*), set in Fingal's Cave, is a fascinating travelogue up Scotland's west coast in the same period.

Jules Verne died in 1905, aged 77, and since his death many of his fantastic predictions in his books — submarines, space travel, television, electric lighting — have come true.

He richly deserves his title 'The Inventor of Science Fiction', but fortunately for the Scottish tourist industry his vision of a coalmine in the Trossachs never came to pass.

The Queen and Muckle Kate

It is likely that Verne also saw one of the unusual attractions of the Trossachs in mid-Victorian times in the shape of Muckle Kate Ferguson, proprietrix of the inn at Brig o' Turk. She was renowned as the fattest woman in the kingdom, weighing over twenty-five stones. She entertained customers with lively conversation in a mixture of Gaelic and English and was noted for her eccentric habit of dropping all monies into a large leather purse fastened to her skirt without giving change. Such was her fame that Queen Victoria paid her a visit in 1868 while staying at nearby Drunkie House. Kate had been given warning of the visit and was standing outside in her finery when the Queen arrived. Her majesty was most interested in her weighty subject and presented her with two sovereigns. This incident made Kate famous throughout the land, and for years afterwards her portrait appeared on postcards in shop windows all over the kingdom.

Less well known is the unfortunate misunderstanding which occurred due to Kate's problems with English. It appears the Queen's party were greatly embarrassed when Kate offered them tea and 'a gill a-piece'. All of them vehemently refused, leaving poor Kate wondering why they did not care for a 'jeely piece', or jam sandwich! Muckle Kate Ferguson died in 1872, and her body was carried in a specially built coffin drawn by a team of horses for burial in Callander old churchyard. The remains of her inn known as the Tigh Mhaide can be seen today forming part of a modernised house by the Brig o' Turk crossroads.

The name of the hamlet derives from Tuirc, a wild boar, for this was a favoured hunting area of the kings of Scotland. It was also a noted area of illicit whisky distilling last century,

The iron eating tree of Brig o' Turk has swallowed a bicycle, an anchor, and numerous pieces of scrap metal, since it was a sapling.

with teams of pack horses bringing the spirit at night to towns and villages.

The Iron Eating Tree

Here today can be seen a curiosity in the form of an iron eating tree which stands by the roadside on the way up to Glen Finglas. It can be seen the tree has completely devoured a bicycle, an anchor, and various other bits of metal and left only their extremities sticking out of the trunk.

The story of this oddity goes back to the late 1930s when a blacksmith, whose premises were adjacent, was giving up business. Various pieces of scrap were flung out into the field and some landed on top of a small sapling. The sapling grew into a large tree and in the process completely encompassed the metal without any apparent ill effects. I have to say it — its bark was obviously no worse for its bike!

CHAPTER 5

Around Doune and the Carse

MacGregor's Oak

No clan suffered like Clan Gregor. They were removed from their ancestral lands in Argyll by an astute legal move by their ambitious neighbours, the Campbells. Turned into outlaws, they were hunted down like animals. The men were butchered for bounty money; their womenfolk branded on the forehead and sent to the Borders as serfs; their children herded into barns to fight like pigs for swill in troughs. Even the very use of their name was forbidden under pain of death for nearly two hundred years.

Only one unknown monument exists to this most unfortunate of Highland clans. It stands in the grounds of Lanrick Castle, near Doune in south Perthshire. This very old estate dates back over 700 years and was held by the Earls of Menteith until 1460 when it was sold to a branch of the Haldanes of Gleneagles, who retained it until the eighteenth century.

The MacGregor monument stands in the middle of a clump of trees on a small hill and is a huge oak tree carved in stone. So lifelike is it that only a close inspection reveals that it differs from its neighbours. This strange edifice takes the form of the MacGregor crest of a broken oak tree, complete with snapped-off branches and scars. Round the top of the stump is a crown with three-foot-high stone points, and rising from these are three pillars supporting a circular platform. From this rises another pillar which once held an acorn. The stone crown proclaims their claimed descent from Griogar, third son of King Alpin in the eighth century, and the clan's slogan, 'My Race is Royal'. The acorn symbolises the clan's rebirth.

114

The whole incredible structure is over sixty feet high, and the covering of moss renders it almost lifelike. The names of the master masons who carved the intricate stonework are unknown but the structure was built between 1800 and 1830.

Lanrick estate was confiscated from the Haldanes for their part in the '45 Uprising and was acquired by a man called Wordie. In 1775, by Act of Parliament, the name MacGregor was permitted to be used again. All over Britain prominent men astounded their peers by throwing off the names their families had been known by for generations, and reverting to MacGregor. One of those was Sir John Murray, a general in the East India Company. He was a nephew of the famous MacGregor of Glencarnaig of the '45, and in 1795 he was recognised as 18th Chief of Clan Gregor.

Sir John Murray MacGregor bought Lanrick and renamed its castle as Castle Gregor. He then erected the curious stone oak tree as a memorial to his clan. Every one of the scars is supposed to represent a member of the clan killed in battle. The second baronet, Sir Evan John MacGregor, sold the estate to William Jardine, founder of the famous Hong Kong trading company of Jardine Matheson, who had made his money in the opium trade. He was the original 'Tai-pan' on whom James Clavell's bestselling novel of that name was based. Sir Evan then built Edinchip House in the old MacGregor lands in Balquhidder, but unfortunately in recent years the present 23rd chief, Sir Gregor MacGregor of MacGregor, sold it and moved away from the district, and now only the mausoleum of the later MacGregor chiefs remains in Balquhidder. It is unfortunate too that the general public cannot view the monument at Lanrick, for the grounds are strictly private.

The Pistol Makers of Doune

The village of Doune, between Stirling and Callander, has two claims to fame. The first is the huge fourteenth-century castle of the Earls of Moray which dominates the town from a defensive knoll above the River Teith. This partially restored ruin is one of the finest example of early Scottish medieval fortification, and featured in many episodes of Scottish history. Today, it is more often remembered in the verses of the popular old ballad, *The Bonnie Earl of Moray:*

> Oh! Lang will his lady
>   Look o'er the Castle of Doune,
> Ere she see the Earl of Moray
>   Come soundin' thro' the toun.

But there is another reason entirely why the name of Doune became renowned not only in Scotland but throughout the known world. For, from this tiny place, came the famous pistols which possessed such mystery, such superb artistry, and such deadly accuracy that they fetched incredible sums in the seventeenth century. Today they are literally worth their weight in gold as collectors' pieces, and many are considered so valuable they are kept only in bank vaults.

The trade of gunmaking started in 1646, shortly after the 6th Earl of Moray had transformed Doune from a miserable collection of cottages clustered round the castle into a well-laid-out burgh, suitable for its role as the centre of civil and criminal law for the ancient Stewartry of Menteith. The Earl also encouraged the holding of fairs and cattle trysts, and soon industries began to flourish, producing wool, leather, dirks, sporrans, brogues and belts. This was not solely for the benefit of the local community, but coincided with the start of the droving of Highland cattle down from the mountains to the Lowland markets. Doune was strategically placed, lying at the intersection of the two great routes from Edinburgh to Inverlochy, and Glasgow to Inverness. The fierce, bearded Highlanders who arrogantly swaggered their way through the town were keen to purchase goods, and

MacGregors' Oak, the only surviving monument to the unfortunate Clan Gregor, lies in the grounds of Lanrick Castle near Doune. Over sixty feet high, the stone tree is incredibly lifelike.

firearms in particular, for the North was still turbulent and warlike.

The guns they bought were mainly manufactured on the East Coast, where high-grade Swedish iron ore was shipped into Leith, Montrose and Dundee to be smelted with coal from East Lothian and Culross. The weapons produced were uniquely Scottish inasmuch as they were generally all-metal, and the butt usually finished in a fish-tail or ball-like form. Although the guns were functional, and had a reasonable degree of accuracy, they compared poorly with the ornate weapons turned out from the workshops of the Continental master-gunsmiths.

However, this situation was to change after a certain Thomas Caddell made his way to Doune in 1646 and set up in business as a gunsmith. He had come from the village of Muthill, some fifteen miles to the north, where he had been a country blacksmith, and it is still a mystery where he acquired his training and rare skill. However, there was a Flemish gunsmith called Cadell working in London at this period who was forced to flee the capital after being accused of an unspecified crime, and this may have been the same man.

Little is known about Caddell as a person, and the only description available is that contained in the *Old Statistical Account* which says: 'this famous tradesman possessed a most profound genius, and an inquisitive mind; and though a man of no education, and remote from every means of instruction in the mechanical arts, his study and perseverance brought his work to so high a degree of perfection that no pistol made in Britain excelled or perhaps equalled those of his making either for sureness or beauty'.

Inquisitive his mind certainly was — for he ignored the traditional and sometimes imprecise forging of his own material. He looked around instead for the surest metal which was easy to work and also in constant supply, and discovered this to be horseshoe nails. His method of using these was ingenious, and it was followed by the generations of Doune pistol makers who succeeded him.

Taking handfuls of nails, he heated and hammered them into a flat slab of metal, then drew this out into a long steel ribbon. This was again heated, and beaten around an iron rod in a close, spiral twist. On some of Caddell's early guns it is possible to see the faint outline of the ribbon. The rod was then withdrawn, and the now roughly shaped barrel was bored out to the correct diameter and the outer surface filed down. The breech end was tapped with a thread and a breech plug screwed in. The lock and mechanism were then closely wrought to the approximate shape, for in those days material was dear and labour cheap, and every ounce of metal was valuable, as were the files which achieved the final finish. The last stage involved working the stock as one piece, and joining it to the barrel before the decoration was applied. It was designed to fire a round lead ball about three-quarters of an inch in diameter.

The end product was an all-steel pistol about fourteen inches long which flowed in perfect symmetry from a ram's head butt to the slight, subtle flaring of the muzzle. It was profusely embellished with scrolls and spirals which are yet another mystery for they are a curious mixture of Oriental and Celtic design, and possess a poetic power of expression which rivals any of the great art treasures.

Although the pistols were works of art, and of a standard rarely found then in Scotland, Caddell designed them initially for the nearest market — the proud and quick-tempered Highlanders — and for this reason they are shorn of safety features. They have no trigger guard or safety catch, have an easy-to-find ball trigger, and were made in pairs for left- or right-hand use. Because of the wild conditions in which they would be used, they were adaptable and functional; the centre knob of the ram's head butt could be quickly unscrewed to form a pricker for the touch hole, and the latter was constructed to hold varying sizes of flint.

Caddell's pistols were soon being eagerly bought by the clansmen, who would gladly pay a lifetime's savings to possess a pair costing between four and twenty guineas. Indeed, some were so proud of their acquisition that they engraved on their powder horns, 'I love thee as my wyfe, I'll keep thee as my lyfe'.

Soon the fame of his guns spread further afield, and in later years more expensive ones were ordered by noble families. These high-quality weapons had inlaid ornamentation of delicate silver and gold wire fused together, which contrasted beautifully with the blue-black colour of the metal. The breech end was fluted, while the touch hole was bushed with gold and the ball-trigger was of silver. A plaque was inserted into the stock for the maker's signature and the coat-

The huge, fourteenth-century Doune Castle on its defensive knoll above the River Teith. It is probably the finest remaining example of early Scottish medieval fortification, and featured in many episodes of Scotland's history.

of-arms of the owner. It was one of Caddell's pistols that the Earl of Argyle was carrying when he was captured crossing the River Cart in 1685, and but for his powder becoming damp he might have escaped his subsequent execution in Edinburgh.

By the beginning of the eighteenth century the weapons had become more sophisticated, and vastly superior to the earlier models, although the method of manufacture remained the same. Caddell passed on his skill to his son and apprentices who, in turn, taught the next generations. Apart from three generations of Caddells, others who are rightly famed include John and Alexander Campbell, Thomas Murdoch, Christie, Bissett and Sutherland. Indeed, these went on to exceed the old master's expertise, and between 1700 and 1800 the manufacture of Doune pistols reached its highest peak with regard to beauty and accuracy.

Caddell's son, Thomas, continued to work in Doune, but his grandson, Robert, established a shop in Edinburgh, and worked there between 1730 and 1764. Alexander Campbell worked in Doune between 1725 and 1775, while three generations of John Campbell's family were active between 1710 and 1798 although latterly not in the village. The last pistol maker to work in Doune, John Murdoch, carried on the trade from 1750 to 1798. From examination of pistols made in Argyll and Mull it is obvious that many unknown gunsmiths also served their apprenticeships in Doune.

Some apprentices, as fully fledged gunsmiths, opened other shops, and that of John Murdoch lay at the corner of Balkerrach Street. The workshop of the Campbell family is said to be incorporated in McAlpine's bakery, on the opposite side of the street from Caddell's, although no identifiable portion is visible.

The beginning of the end for the pistol makers started with the destruction of the very people for whom the guns were first made — the Highland clansmen. This would have seemed unbelievable in the autumn of 1745 when Bonnie Prince Charlie's army marched through Newton of Doune on its way south to disaster. Pistols hung from the belts of the better-armed clansmen, attached by an inbuilt hook, while those on horseback carried them in saddle holsters (the guns weighed over eight pounds).

When the army stopped to allow Prince Charlie to 'pree the mou" of the fair Clementina Edmonstone, one can imagine the gunsmiths hurrying from their shops to gaze with pride at their work, or that of their fathers or grandfathers, as over a hundred years of pistol-making skill was exhibited in its birthplace.

But the subsequent crushing of the '45 Uprising, and the passing of the Disarmament Act, meant that the traditional market was finished for good. The gunsmiths began to export to England and the Continent, and the workmanship entered its finest period. Every European capital knew of them, and of their cost which now exceeded fifty guineas. Kings and nobles boasted when they acquired a pair, and ignored their own beautifully engraved coats-of-arms as they gazed with pride at the signature of Caddell, Campbell or Murdoch.

Ferdinand, Prince of Brunswick, had a pair, as had the Duke of Cumberland, and they were considered the finest gift one could give. A superb medallion-encrusted pair was given to Lord Cornwallis by George III, and such presentation pistols can be identified by the decoration being 'applied' to the guns rather than part of them.

Today, pistols from Doune are displayed in almost every principal museum on the Continent, and the oldest such weapon is one of 1678, signed by Thomas Caddell, in the Neuchâtel Museum in Switzerland. Perhaps the finest of all is the gold-engraved pair in the Armoury of Windsor Castle, although many beautiful examples can be seen in the National Museums of Scotland in Queen Street, Edinburgh.

Many of the later pistols found their way to America, and it was a gun sold by John Murdoch to a Major Pitcairn that fired the first shot in the American War of Independence. This officer set out to confiscate colonial gunpowder at Concord, but his overnight march on April 19, 1775, was forestalled by the celebrated ride of Paul Revere. Pitcairn arrived at Lexington to find himself confronted by American Minutemen. He drew his pistols and fired, but a hail of bullets killed him. His pistols are now preserved in Lexington Museum.

The trade began to die out towards the end of the eighteenth century following the mass production of cheap Birmingham imitations. The Great Banqueting Hall at Edinburgh Castle is hung with scores of pistols which appear at first sight to be authentic; unfortunately a close examination shows the name of an English firm, and the proof marks of Birmingham, for these were issued in great numbers to the Scottish regiments at a cost of eighteen shillings a pair.

Around this time many of the old gunmaking families began to leave Doune to work in the major cities. One of the Murdochs who had settled in Leith applied for the post of gunsmith to the Board of Ordnance. This superb craftsman

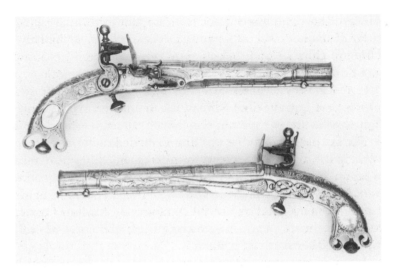

A standard pair of Doune pistols made by John Murdoch, 1750—1798, the last of the traditional gunsmiths. Among their unique features were the lack of a trigger guard, the large ball trigger, the ram's head butt, and their construction from horseshoe nails. Photo: Sotheby's Ltd.

was turned down on the grounds that he 'had only been used to making Highland pistols'.

The *Old Statistical Account* sounded the epitaph in 1798. 'There is now,' it states, 'little demand for Doune pistols owing to the low price of pistols made in England; but the chief reason for the decline is the disuse of the dirk and pistols as part of Caledonian dress; and when Mr. Murdoch gives over business, the trade, in all probability, will become extinct'.

The tartan revival fostered by Sir Walter Scott's novels, and George IV's Scottish visit, arrived too late. By the time the over-enthusiastic Victorians were donning all manner of extraordinary tartan garb for evening wear, the 'genuine Highland pistols' they carried were simply costume weapons made from light, composition metal in London or Birmingham. Regrettably, the clan chiefs depicted in Sir

Henry Raeburn's superb portraits are shown to be wearing these imitations, and only paintings done before 1800 portray authentic pistols.

All that now remains in Doune is Caddell's old workshop and the graves of generations of pistol makers in the old overgrown graveyard of Kilmadock about a mile to the west. But the beauty of the weapons they created, described by a French expert as 'leaving nothing to be desired on the score of balance, form, or decoration', lives on. They are rare works of art, and anyone fortunate to find one, and perhaps read on the plaque *Jno. Campbell Duni Fecit* (Made in Doune by John Campbell) has indeed discovered a treasure. Apart from the pleasure in owning such a pistol, they currently sell for many thousands of pounds.

John Blackwood, a Doune antique dealer, has restored Caddell's old pistol factory in recent years. During the work a Highland broadsword was discovered hidden in the roof, perhaps a relic from the Disarmament Act in the aftermath of the '45 Uprising.

The Moss Lairds

The River Forth marks the southern boundary of Perthshire. The flood plain it winds through, the Carse of Stirling, has been aptly called the Moat of Scotland. A great glacier once gouged out the valley of the Forth, and when it melted, the sea came rushing in to reach as far as Gartmore, near Aberfoyle. Then the land rose and the sea receded, leaving behind a semi-fluid, quaking peat bog four miles wide by fourteen miles long. Through this flood plain meandered the slow coils of the Forth, falling less than twelve feet in as many miles. The swamp it traversed was totally impassable over most of its 35,000 acres, and the only way a large body of men could cross it was by means of the bridge and causeway at Stirling. Little wonder the castle here was called the Key to the Kingdom, for whoever held it, held all Scotland.

In later years, the only people who could traverse the Carse in all weathers were the MacGregors who used secret tracks and hidden causeways to escape back into the Highlands after raids on the Lowlands. None dared follow them into the bottomless marsh.

There was, however, one route which was passable in very dry weather, and this led from Kincardine in Menteith to the Ford of Frew on the Forth. The Marquis of Montrose used it in 1645 when he unexpectedly brought his nimble-footed Highland army south to win the battle of Kilsyth. A hundred years later, Prince Charles Edward Stuart also led a Highland army across it to avoid Stirling Castle.

Apart from this summer crossing, the Carse remained an impenetrable, quaking peat bog covered with dense marsh vegetation, inhabited only by wildfowl and the most desperate of outlaws. It remained like this until 1766 when Agatha Drummond inherited the ancestral estate of Blair Drummond on the north side of the Carse about five miles from Stirling. Her family took its name from their original barony of Drymen, and Agatha was married to the learned, but eccentric, Henry Home, Lord Kames, a judge of the Court of Session. His outspoken remarks shocked even hardened eighteenth-century Edinburgh society. He is renowned for his comment during a court case — 'My Lords, I like fine the lassies', and for his parting words to his fellow Lords of Session — 'Fareweel, ye bitches!'

He was over 70 when he and his wife took up residence at Blair Drummond. They found that over 1500 acres of the soaking moss lay within the inherited estate and he turned his undoubted intellect towards the problem of draining it. Beneath the moss lay rich, alluvial clay which would produce fertile and valuable farmland. Workmen were employed to carry out various experiments, and he finally proved that a stream of water, of sufficient force to turn a corn mill, could carry off as much moss as twenty men, each stationed a hundred yards apart, could throw into it. The ideal size of drain was found to be two feet by two feet. Any narrower,

E

The restored pistol factory of Thomas Caddell at Doune.

and it would not receive a spadeful of moss, any deeper, and the water would drain away.

Lord Kames found an ideal source in the water being led from the River Teith to drive a corn mill at the Mill of Torr. He paid the tenant compensation, and pulled it down. Then he cut a three-mile channel right across the Carse, from Blair Drummond to the Forth, with a fall of 1 in 300, and diverted the mill lade into it. He now had the method and the basic principles to begin draining the moss; to continue with hired workmen, however, would prove too costly.

Kames advertised for tenants in the Callander area and offered them a lease of eight acres for thirty-eight years. They were to be provided with timber to build a house and enough oatmeal to sustain them for a year. They would pay no rent for seven years; in the eighth, one merk; in the ninth, two merks; and thereafter they would pay 12s for each cleared acre and 2/6d for each acre of moss. This was quite a bargain when the best farmland at this time had a rent of 30s.

In 1768, the first tenant was settled on the Low Moss, nearest to Blair Drummond, and by 1774 another eleven were established. The moss here was only three feet thick, and the new settlers quickly stripped this off and flung it into the slow-moving channel to be washed down to the Forth.

Within a year, the first crops had been produced, and when Lord Kames died in 1783, aged 86, some twenty-nine tenants were living on 400 acres of cleared moss.

His son, George Home Drummond, continued his father's project but had to find new methods. The remaining 1100 acres, comprising the High Moss and the Flow Moss, lay nearer the centre of the Carse. It was over twelve feet deep in the first section, but on the Flow Moss it was bottomless. A man could not walk here unless he wore boards on his feet to spread his weight, and a stamp of the foot made the moss quake for fifty yards.

George Meikle of Alloa was commissioned to design a pumping wheel which would lift the mill lade through seventeen feet, and pump the water faster. Meikle produced a remarkable invention in the shape of a wheel ten feet wide and twenty-eight feet in diameter. It was designed to lift six tons of water seventeen feet every minute, and to be powered by the same water. To this end it was fitted with eighty buckets and worked by an ingenious system of sluices. George Home Drummond then consulted with a Mr. Whitworth, superintendent of the London waterworks and lately an engineer of the new Forth and Clyde Canal.

Whitworth devised a series of channels, branches and reservoirs which would criss-cross the whole area. Meikle's wheel pumped the water to a cistern which discharged into 400 yards of underground wooden pipes, then into an aqueduct, and from there the fast-moving water spread out through the system. It was designed to fill the reservoirs of one section during the day, and another at night. The cost was over £1000, and the work was carried out by contractors.

A special breed of person was now required who could

endure the hardship of living on the moss. Home Drummond found them amongst the poverty-stricken, dispossessed Highlanders of Perthshire who were still suffering from the consequences of the Jacobite Uprising fifty years before. Most came from the Balquhidder area, but one family, my great-great-great-grandfather's, came from Glen Lyon. Peter and Elizabeth McArrichar arrived with their family at Blair Drummond in 1793, and were allocated Plot 15 in Kirk Lane. This was a sunken twelve-foot-wide road dug down to the clay and crossing the Carse between twelve-foot-high walls of peat and moss. It is now the B8075.

The eight-acre plot was marked off and behind it ran a drainage channel connected with the complex of waterways. It was summer, and the whole family set to work stripping the top three-foot layer of sphagnum moss which they flung into the ditch. Then came their house. On a small area beside the road, they proceeded to clear the next three-foot layer which consisted of swamp grass and rotting vegetation. Once down to the layer of peat, they cut four trenches about five feet deep right down into the clay sub-strata. Then they scooped out the interior like a turnip lantern. The outside walls dried and shrank, and the estate timber was used to form a roof over this pit which was covered with turf.

Others were not so fortunate. In some areas, the moss was so soft that the houses had to be built on boards and literally floated on top.

Soon over a hundred little houses had been built and the whole area was covered with people toiling to strip off as much moss as possible before the winter. It was appalling work, for they were soaked from morning to night, and there was little comfort inside the rude huts. However, being Highlanders, they were used to living in the harshest of conditions.

Every so often, a great flood of water was sent sweeping along the channels from the great wheel two miles away and the moss, vegetation and peat was washed down to the Forth.

The lease conditions were different here because of the

immense problems. The tack was still for thirty-eight years, but no rent was payable for the first nineteen.

The local farmers did everything possible to obstruct the work, and the surrounding population ostracised the new settlers and mockingly referred to them as The Moss Lairds. The newcomers eked out an isolated life in what was virtually a loch colony. They spoke only Gaelic and thus were unable to attend the local church or have their children educated.

An appeal was made to the Society for the Propagation of Christian Knowledge for a teacher-cum-missionary, but this was refused at first because they were not residing in the Highlands. Eventually, George Home Drummond offered the Society a subsidy of £5 per annum and a Gaelic-speaking teacher was established in a school on the moss in 1795.

The Home Drummonds did everything possible to encourage their new tenants. A prize of a new plough was offered to the one who had cleared the largest area in a year. A new metalled road was driven in from the east (now the A84), and so grateful were the tenants that they offered £100 towards the cost, but this was declined. The estate ensured that nobody went hungry or was ill-clothed, and even arranged the services of a doctor. Apart from the wet conditions, it seems to have been a healthy enough life, for the antiseptic properties of the peat and moss kept most diseases at bay. The mortality rate amongst children was certainly high, but mainly as a result of croup and smallpox.

A brick and tile works was built on the west side of Kirk Lane, using the exposed clay as raw material. Soon, neat houses of brick walls and tiled roofs had replaced the earlier huts once the clay foundation had been reached, and the areas immediately adjacent to the roads began to have a prosperous appearance. Several strange discoveries were made during the drainage. The entire skeleton of a whale was uncovered at the top of Kirk Lane, as were several brass cooking pots believed to be of Roman origin. The most interesting find was on the east boundary, at Drip Moss, where a floating road was unearthed, formed by huge tree trunks bound together with a layer of brushwood on top. This was believed to be Roman, but was the subject of much speculation as the Roman road north was supposed to run much closer to Stirling.

A recent dry summer enabled Dr. St. Joseph of the Department of Aerial Photography at Cambridge University to locate an unknown Roman marching camp of the first century on the hill above Blair Drummond. Thus it was proved that the legions crossed the Carse on a floating road which ran in a north-west direction.

A detailed census of the population on the moss was carried out in 1811 and this showed 764 men, women and children living there along with 264 cows, 166 horses, 375 hens, 30 pigs, 168 cats and eight dogs! Things were improving each year as more and more land was cleared. Once the peat layer was reached, the settlers sold this for fuel in neighbouring towns, and began producing crops. The great wheel at the Mill of Torr turned continuously for sixty-one years until, by 1840, all the area had been cleared right down to the clay. It was a stupendous operation. At a rough calculation, over twenty million cubic yards of moss, vegetation, and ancient tree trunks had been excavated solely by human power.

By 1840, the original leases had expired, and the only criticism of the project was that the tenants were then left with nothing. However, many had sold their leases at a profit once their plots were cleared, and used the money to buy farms elsewhere. Many also put in bids to amalgamate several of the plots into larger units, and out of the fifty or so houses ranged along Kirk Lane, only two farms exist today.

The majority of the original tenants drifted off the moss on the expiry of their leases. My great-grandfather remained till 1850. One of his sons, my great-grand uncle, moved to Stirling to become a prosperous merchant and owner of the Raploch Farm below the castle until it was sold to the Town Council in 1927 for the present housing scheme.

Other landowners followed the example of the Home Drummonds. Graham of Meiklewood employed a ten-

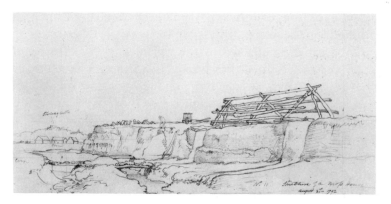

The moss lairds' houses were formed by placing a roof of timber on the peat bog and digging out the interior. This contemporary sketch of 1792 shows the sunken road cut through the swamp, now the B8075. The house illustrated may have been that of the author's ancestors. Photo: The Royal Commission on the Ancient & Historical Monuments of Scotland.

horsepower steam engine to clear his 150 acres south of the Blair Drummond lands from 1840 onwards. Several schemes were started further west to reclaim some of the vast Flanders Moss, but all such work was prohibited in 1865 as the peat and moss had silted up the Forth at Stirling and finished it as a sea port. Oyster beds and salmon runs were also ruined.

The foreshore of the Forth as far down as Bo'ness and Culross was littered with peat blocks which local farmers carted off for their fields. However, by this time over 10,000 acres of the Carse of Stirling, stretching eight miles west from the Castle, had been turned into fertile farmland.

The Home Drummond family sold the estate in 1912 to Sir John Muir of the world-famous tea firm, James Finlay & Company. In recent years, the present Sir John has sold the mansionhouse of Blair Drummond to the Camphill Trust, while the grounds are the renowned Safari Park. The Carse of Stirling today is a flat, fertile area famous for its dairy cattle and the production of Timothy grass, much valued as hill fodder.

Some of the complex of ditches and channels which drained the Carse are still visible today.

Opposite the entrance to the Safari Park is an area of woodland called the Ochtertyre Moss. Although much drier than in years past, it is a living example of how this whole area once looked, and on its south side it drops dramatically by eight feet to the flat of the carse.

If you want to see exactly what it was like, then travel west to the vast area of Flanders Moss which remains an untamed, undrained area of nearly twenty square miles.

Henry Home, Lord Kames, and his son George Home Drummond, lie in the little graveyard of Kincardine in Menteith at the top of Kirk Lane. Beside them lie the Moss Lairds who left their Highland homes to begin a new and strange life on the bog. The ingenuity of the former, and the arduous work of the latter, turned a useless swamp into the fertile land they watch over today.

Heather Jock

But to turn now from the good to the bad, and there was none worse than Heather Jock. His fame, and his eventual fate, attracted scores of imitators in the early nineteenth century, and many 'Heather Jocks' are described throughout Scotland. The original, however, was quite unique, and the first verse of a ballad describes him vividly:

> Heather Jock was stark and grim,
> Faucht wi aa wad fecht wi him;
> Swank[1] and supple, sharp and thin,   [1]lithe
> Fine for gaun against the win'.
> Tawny face and towsy hair,
> In his cleedin[2] unco bare.   [2]clothing
> Cursed and swore when'er he spoke,
> Nane could equal Heather Jock.

His real name was John Fergusson, born in 1780 in a small, thatched cottage in the grounds of Newton House, Doune, beside the old road to Dunblane. Jock's father died when he was young and the family moved to a wretched hovel beside the Smuggler's Road, high up on the moors above Kilbryde, between the farms of Dalbrack and Towrie.

Kilbryde is a rural area lying to the north of the main Dunblane/Doune road. Today it is sparsely populated with farms' and estate workers' cottages, and comprises flat farmland rising to high moorland. At its centre is the fifteenth-century Kilbryde Castle, the seat for 300 years of the Campbells of Aberuchill and Kilbryde.

But in 1800, a mere forty-five years before the dramatic changes wrought by the coming of the railway, Kilbryde was a bustling, densely populated and self-contained community. The folk were honest, hard-working and God-fearing, with one exception — Heather Jock!

In modern parlance, Heather Jock would be described as an underprivileged, single-parent child from a deprived, socio-economic background. Some have risen from such circumstances to become prime ministers, rulers of men and captains of industry. Jock, however, grew up a loner, a tall, gangly, ill-kept body who terrorised the neighbourhood:

> Jock was nae religious youth,
> At the priest he thraw'd his mooth,
> He wadna say a grace or pray,
> But played his pipes on Sabbath day.

Needless to say, Heather Jock became a dreaded thief and poacher.

Various reasons have been given for his nickname. Some say it was because his shaggy, unkempt hair resembled a heather besom. More likely it arose because skulking in the heather was his natural habitat. He stole everything from anybody.

> Jock kent ilka bore and bole,
> Could creep through a wee bit hole,
> Quietly pilfer eggs an cheese,
> Dunts a bacon, skeps o bees;
> Sip the kirn and steal the butter
> Nail the hens without a flutter;
> Na! The watchful wily cock,
> Durstna craw for Heather Jock.

His thefts were not confined to food, for —

> Eppie Blaikie lost her gown,
> She cost sae dear in burgh town;
> Sandy Tamson's Sunday wig,
> Left the house to run the rig;
> Jenny Baxter's blankets aa,
> Took a thocht to run awa;
> E'en the wean's bit printed frock,
> Wha was thief — but Heather Jock?

He was also an expert poacher who

> Watched the wild ducks at the springs,
> And hanged the hares in hempen strings.

Few dared cross him, though, for Heather Jock was a deadly shot. He would invariably carry off the best prizes at the Hansel Monday shooting matches, leaving the locals to glare and mutter amongst themselves. He was so notorious that the entire population of Dunblane turned out to watch when he came to buy shot. The children screamed with fright at the sight of the grim, lanky figure slinking along the street, and clutched their mothers' skirts, for the threat held over them was, 'Be good, or Heather Jock'll get ye!'

The local gamekeepers feared him, too, for when

> Keepers catch'd him on the muir,
> Kickit up an uncou stour;
> Charged him to lay doun his gun.

The channels used to drain the Carse are still visible running through the now flat and fertile fields. The original ground level here was twelve feet higher. In the background is Blair Drummond House.

> Or his nose should delve the grun.
> Jock slipp'd doun ahint a hurst,
> Cried, 'Ye swabs, I'll empty first';
> They saw his fingers at the lock,
> And left the field to Heather Jock,

Once, on Slymaback Hill, he was challenged by his own cousin, John Drummond, keeper to Patrick Stirling of Kippendavie. Despite their relationship, Jock fired at him, and only the extreme distance caused the ball to thud harmlessly into the turf at the keeper's feet.

Not surprisingly, the community ostracised Jock and his mother. The poor woman, unable to bear the shame and her miserable existence, hanged herself from the cottage rafters. Jock cut her down and kept the rope as a memento. He used

it shortly after to lead home a stolen cow, whose rightful
owners came in hot pursuit. Jock blandly invited them to
search his house, but they found nothing. They were about
to retire baffled, when they heard a faint mooing from
indoors. They searched again, and found the hapless cow
squashed into a wall recess behind a press bed. How Jock got
it in is a mystery because it took six men to get it out! Jock
made no attempt to interfere until the angry men were about
to set out for home. Quite calmly, he asked if he might have
the rope back as it reminded him of his mother.

This trend to larger thefts led to his undoing. In December
1810, he went to Stirling, where, in an inn, he met a stranger
called MacCallum. That night, the pair went to the nearby
estate of Gartur and stole two fat cows which they drove to
Glasgow. Jock sold them for £20 but was immediately
apprehended by Graham of Gartur's servants who had followed
them. They took him back, and Jock poured out such a story
of his tragic youth that the kindly Mr. Graham agreed to
Jock's suggestion that he would serve aboard a ship of war if
he was spared a trial. He was taken next day to *H.M.S.
Adamant* in Leith Roads, but was abroad only two nights
before he deserted and made his way back home.

He seemed to have tried briefly to mend his ways by
spending the summer of 1811 as a weaver in Menteith and
Menstrie. During this period he devoted his spare time to
music — he was an expert fiddler — and to making clocks.
These timepieces were made entirely from wood, even the
cogs, and some still survive.

Old habits die hard, however, and in the autumn of that
year, he stole a red cow from Hugh MacLean of Daldorn in
Menteith. He sold it to his own brother-in-law, a farmer at
Gartcraig near Bannockburn.

This time he had gone too far. He was arrested and brought
before the High Court when it came to Stirling in April
1812. Jock was charged with the theft of Mr. Graham's two
cows; Mr. MacLean's red cow; four hares from Drumawhinnance

The remains of Heather Jock's 'bit hoosie in the glen' are still visible on the moors above Kilbryde.

which he had sold to the guard of the Glasgow-Perth coach; and a large pointer dog belonging to Mrs. Cunninghame-Graham of Gartmore.

His indictment bluntly refers to him as a known thief and poacher, but his occupation was recorded as the rather unusual combination of 'Weaver and Dog Breeder'. His full name is given only once, and thereafter he is referred to by his nickname, which indicates just how notorious he was.

He was found guilty and sentenced to transportation for life to Botany Bay. It is said that his shackles were forged by the Kilbryde smith, perhaps to let the local people see that justice had been done.

Needless to say, Heather Jock was no ordinary transportee. It is said he escaped from the dreaded prison hulk moored in the Thames and was recaptured in Edinburgh while trying to sell two fine dogs belonging to the prison commandant.

He finally sailed aboard the *Earl Spencer* on 2nd June, 1813, and arrived at Sydney, Australia on 9th October, 1813, some eighteen months after being convicted at Stirling. The ship's papers describe him as a weaver, height about 5 feet 2½ inches, with a ruddy complexion, brown hair and hazel eyes. Religion Protestant.

I had often wondered about Heather Jock's eventual fate in the grim convict colony. Thanks to a fine piece of research by Mr. A. W. Flynn, late of Linlithgow and now in New South Wales, Australia, the remainder of Jock's life is known. It seems he married a fellow convict, Christabella Ogle, and they had three children, two of whom died young. He applied for and was granted a ticket of leave in 1818 which allowed him to work for himself outwith the convict gangs, and in the first census of 1828 he is found working for a Scots minister, the Rev. Dr. Lang.

Jock's wife died in 1836 aged 52 and Jock seems to have gone downhill. His son John was also now a convict and sold land which legally was not his. The police magistrate described John and his son as objectionable characters but no court case developed. Heather Jock was granted a conditional pardon in July, 1848, after serving in the prison colony for thirty-five years. This allowed him to travel anywhere in the world except the United Kingdom. He died six years later in mysterious circumstances after disappearing in April, 1854. His body was found two years later on General MacArthur's estate at Parammatta, and the inquest suggested a possible accident.

Heather Jock might have disappeared into oblivion after leaving Scotland except that a Dr. James Stirling, born at The Biggins near Dunblane, immortalised him in a ballad. Stirling had been about ten years old when Heather Jock was in his heyday, and had probably run in terror on many occasions on seeing the grim figure skulking along the hedgerows. James Stirling emigrated to Canada after graduating as a doctor in 1820. He settled at Caledonia

Springs, Ontario, where he published a local paper and wrote many poetical pieces. The final verse to the ballad provided the moral message beloved by the Victorians:

> Jock's bit housie i'the glen
> Lies in ruins, but an ben;
> There the mawkin safe may rest
> And the muirfowl build her nest.
> Ower the sea Jock's herdin' swine,
> Glad wi' them on husks to dine;
> Sae tak warning, honest folk —
> Never do like Heather Jock.

CHAPTER 6

The Devil, the Prince, and the Flower of Dunblane

The Devil and Clanranald

'Some say that they won, and some say that we won, and some say that nane won at a'', says an old ballad about the inconclusive battle of Sheriffmuir in 1715. But the battle also saw the climax of a strange, supernatural mystery which began far away at Castle Tiorim in Moidart. This gaunt, grim keep perched on a rocky, tidal islet was built by Amie MacRuari, divorced wife of John mhic Dhomhail, Lord of the Isles, in 1358. Her second son Ranald was the founder of the Clanranald division of the House of Donald and his patrimony was the islands of Uist, Benbecula, and Eigg and the lands of Moidart, Knoydart, Morar and Arisaig on the mainland, known in Gaelic as the Garbh Criochan, The Rough Bounds.

Castle Tiorim became the seat of the chiefs of Clanranald and many are the tales of this stormy, warlike race. Dugall the Cruel, 6th chief, was killed by his own clansmen for his atrocities. The blood of one of his victim's, done to death in a particularly horrible way, can still be seen on Tiorim's dungeon floor.

But the strange story related here concerns Donald mhic Dhomhill who became 12th chief in 1670 at the age of 46. His greatest joy was his Spanish long gun called The Cuckoo with which he used to take pot shots from the battlements. He was thus occupied one day when he noticed a suspicious character lurking near his sheep on the mainland. Donald took aim and fired, and saw his victim fall head first into a well. His ghillies ran to the spot and returned with the sad news that the chief had killed one of his most faithful servants, known as the Lad of the Wet Feet. It had been his duty to walk through the heather in front of Donald to ensure not a drop of moisture touched his master's feet. Donald declared, 'If the lad was innocent of trying to remove my sheep then I've removed him from temptation. But if he was guilty then he got what he deserved!'

Then there was the time when a sum of money went missing from the castle. Donald tied a suspected maidservant by her hair to a tidal rock until she drowned, and the rock is still marked on maps as The Rock of James's Daughter. As the girl failed to confess, Donald then hanged a ghillie who also was unable to enlighten him. (In fact, the money was found under a rock opposite the castle during road-building operations late last century.) Donald's old cook was foolish enough to take not only a pinch of his snuff but also the snuffbox itself. She too was promptly hanged.

It was obvious that one with Donald's natural wickedness would attract the Powers of Darkness. The manifestation came in the form of a huge and hideous toad which hopped up to Donald one day and nestled by his side. He fed it on milk and meat until it grew to enormous size and followed him everywhere. The clansmen were terrified of the creature which quite clearly was the Devil's emissary. Donald eventually went to desperate lengths to free himself. On one occasion he locked the toad in the dungeon and sailed away in his galley only to find it swimming after him. Another time he again fled by sea but found the creature waiting for him at the jetty on Uist. He was now known as Black Donald of the Toad and was such a promising pupil that the Devil himself came for him in death. As he lay dying on Canna in 1686, a shrill whistle was heard all over the island at midnight. Donald tried to jump from his deathbed but was restrained by his cousin, Ranald Mac Ailean Oig. The terrified ghillies saw a tall, black Person with long pointed ears standing on a rock overlooking the house. The Thing stamped its foot impatiently and roared with fury at its summons being unanswered. Once again Donald tried to leave but was held by his cousin who had studied how to combat the Evil One at Padua University. A desperate battle went on until the first cock crowed and Donald shook his cousin's hand gratefully and slipped away to Tir Nan Og. The Dark Person outside, balked of its promised soul, gave a roar of anger and leapt from the cliff into the sea.

So what has this strange tale to do with Dunblane in Perthshire? Well, it is quite obvious that the Devil had a score to settle with the House of Clanranald. Allan *Dearg* succeeded his father as 13th chief and brought out Clan Ranald in 1715 for the Jacobite Uprising of that year. He was recruiting in South Uist when a Wise Woman cast a protective charm on him. She immediately regretted her action when Allan insisted her sixteen-year-old son must go with him to fight. She implored him to leave the boy who was her sole support, but Allan was insistent. The Speywife vowed Allan would never return and handed her son a bent coin. 'Here is a crooked sixpence, seven times cursed. Let it avail you in battle against Little Allan to break my Charm. Do this, or you will have my curse upon your head!' The terrified boy took the coin, and set out with his chief and six hundred island clansmen for the mainland.

Allan *Dearg* also had a premonition he would not return and ordered Castle Tiorim set alight. He watched from Glenfinnan as a tall column of smoke rose into the sky, then led a thousand fighting men south. Castle Tiorim has remained a ruin from that day to this.

The Jacobite army assembled at Perth and after several false starts the Jacobite leader, the Earl of Mar, finally brought his Highland army south. At 6.30 a.m. on 13th November, 1715, the Jacobite forces comprising ten thousand men were drawn up in two lines on the Moor of Kinbuck, a mile or so north-west of Dunblane. The Government army of around three thousand, commanded by the Duke of Argyll, was stationed around Stonehill Farm south-east of the town while the Duke was on top of the ridge peering

These large heather-covered mounds in front of The Gathering
Stone on Sheriffmuir are the mass graves of the Jacobites killed at
the battle on 13th November, 1715.

down into the dark and misty valley below. Nothing
happened until 11 a.m. when the Jacobites split into two
columns. One of these came straight uphill towards the
Duke who hastily ordered his cavalry to move further up.
The Highlanders came pouring over the crest and down
onto the flat ground around Leys farm. Normally this was
marshland but the severity of the frost had rendered the
ground rock hard. This was ideal for the heavy cavalry,
mainly consisting of the Scots Greys, and they smashed the
Highlanders back over the summit. The dead were placed in
heaps and earth dug over them. The great burial mounds
are still visible beside The Gathering Stone where tradition
claims the Duke of Argyll stood watching.

But further downhill quite the reverse was happening.
The MacDonalds were part of the Jacobite right column
which moved along the base of the hill until it met with the

143

infantry left wing of the Government army. As usual an exchange of gunfire took place. The bullets were flying thick and fast around Allan *Dearg* of Clanranald who, although the only mounted Highlander, remained miraculously unscathed. The Wise Woman's son watched in mounting dread as he had hoped an enemy would do what he dared not. But eventually his fear of his mother's curse overcame his loyalty to his chief. He placed the bent sixpence in his flintlock, took careful aim, and fired. Allan *Dearg* MacDonald toppled from his horse mortally wounded and his clansmen gathered round weeping and lamenting. MacDonald of Glengarry rounded on them fiercely. '*Tomorrow* for weeping!' he cried out savagely in Gaelic. '*Today* for revenge!', and the entire Clan Donald hurled itself at the left wing of the Government army and within five minutes had put it to flight. However, due to the contours of the land neither commander knew what had happened to his respective wings. Eventually the Earl of Mar brought back his victorious right wing of around four thousand men and the Duke of Argyll brought back the one thousand of *his* right wing. The sides stood facing each other until 5 p.m. when Argyll took his troops off the field. In the morning he sent out to collect the wounded but the patrols discovered the Jacobite army had drifted away northwards, and Argyll claimed the victory.

Allan *Dearg* MacDonald of Clanranald was carried away to Drummond Castle near Crieff where he died and was buried at Innerpeffray Chapel close by. Now, the history books say he was hit in the chest by a Hanoverian bullet and of course there is no mention of such a foolish notion as the boy from South Uist and his mother's curse. This might be dismissed as folklore — except that when Allan's grave was opened late last century it was found the skull was split — as though he had been hit by an irregular shaped object, like a bent sixpence!

But in one way I suppose the Devil did finally settle accounts with the House of Clanranald for Reginald George,

20th chief, dissipated his patrimony in the gaming salons of London. He was forced to sell off all the ancestral lands between 1811 and 1837, and spent the next thirty years bitterly regretting the follies of his youth. Only Castle Tiorim on its rock remains to the present chief of Clanranald.

Dunblane and the '45

Thousands of words have been written about the Jacobite Uprising of 1745, which was a much more serious affair than the '15. Hundreds of historians have pondered on what might have been if this or that decision had been made. But nobody ever mentions the humble serving girl from Dunblane who nearly altered the course of history all by herself.

On the afternoon of 11th September, 1745, the Highland army of Prince Charles Edward Stuart entered the small town at the start of its fated march south into England. The army comprised just 2400 ill-disciplined and ragged clansmen — a pitifully small number to restore a Royal dynasty to its rightful inheritance. They came by the old main road, built on top of the Roman road, which runs parallel to the modern A9. No doubt many glanced eastwards to the slopes of Sheriffmuir where the first Jacobite Uprising of 1715 had collapsed.

The town they were entering was a poor place of around a thousand poverty-stricken inhabitants. The houses were mainly crude stone cottages with thatched roofs coming down to within five feet of the ground. Families lived in one room and their livestock in the other, while the refuse of both was flung into the streets. 'Dirty Dumblane! Let us pass it by!' wrote an English traveller in 1694 — for the town had fallen far from its previous grandeur. The sole reason for its existence had been its magnificent cathedral, built between 1240 and 1300. And the only reason for a cathedral in the first place had been King David I's desire to suppress what

Balhaldie House, Dunblane, the town house of MacGregor of Balhaldie. The original part is furthest away. Here Prince Charles Edward Stuart spent the night of 11th September 1745.

was then a major foundation of the old Celtic or Columban church. This had been established in A.D. 604 by the Irish missionary St. Blane, and from him, and his headquarters in an old Pictish dun, or hill fort, behind the town, had come the town's name.

Dunblane had reached the peak of its prosperity and prestige in 1500 when James IV elevated it to the status of a City. The king made secret visits here to see his secret wife, Margaret Drummond, and their daughter, and almost every prince of church and state maintained a mansion in the town. The Bishops lived regally in their huge palace beside the cathedral and administered a vast diocese which covered most of south Perthshire and part of Fife. But the Reformation of the mid-sixteenth century enabled local landowners to seize back the church lands their ancestors had gifted over the centuries. The new Protestant church had no income, and without funds to support it the cathedral had crumbled into a partial ruin by 1588. The local infrastructure had also collapsed, and Dunblane was noted only for handloom weaving and illicit trafficking in spirits and tobacco.

However, the town appeared a veritable paradise to the half-starved clansmen whose normal diet was brackish mutton and raw oatmeal, and whose houses were primitive hovels. They quickly dispersed to seek out loot, despite the Prince's orders to the contrary. Many of the local people supported the Jacobite cause but their rebukes were answered jeeringly by some of the clansmen who declared they fought 'neither for King Shordy nor King Hamish but for King Spulzie' (King George, King James and King Plunder). A single Highlander gained access to a lonely croft above the town by threatening to burn it over the head of its aged, woman occupant. She watched in despair as he leaned far inside her meal barrel to scour it clean, for she faced starvation without her meagre supply to see her through the winter. In desperation she tipped him in head first and held his flailing legs until he expired. One party of Highlanders found a full meal barrel in a cottage in the suburb of Ramoyle and bolted the door lest others follow. Those left outside hammered for admittance with the muzzles of their Spanish muskets, and the marks they made can be seen today for the door is preserved in Dunblane's cathedral museum.

Prince Charles and his generals, oblivious to the mayhem in the streets, took up residence in Balhaldie House, the town house of Alexander Drummond, or MacGregor, the leading Jacobite agent and chief of that outlawed clan. Here the Prince held an evening reception attended by most of the ladies of the town, whose sympathies were with the Stuarts, and who swooned over the tall, handsome and romantic Prince with his strong Italian accent. But while he charmed the ladies, their menfolk, who were mainly Hanoverians, were fighting desperately to prevent their houses being stripped bare. They were aided by a Jacobite provo-marshal, 'an auld man wi kilt and tap-boots, mountit on a black heelan filly', and several of his officers applied the flat of their swords to the looters as they ran from door to door.

The Prince woke early next morning and found a serving girl kneeling by his bed. She had stayed awake all night to polish his boots and to watch over him. Not daring to touch his outstretched hands, she kissed one of his boots instead, and hugged it to her. She was crying openly and the Prince tried to cheer her. 'Ah, but my Prince, my Prince', sobbed the girl, 'but there's ten to one against you!' With those prophetic words ringing in his ears Prince Charles mounted his white horse — and had a purse of gold pressed into his hands by the wife of the chief Baillie. His ragged army, heavily laden with booty, was slowly assembled, and the Prince led his small force out of Dunblane along the old road to Doune. From here they crossed the watery swamp of the Carse of Stirling by the Ford of Frew, and headed south into England. They were only one hundred miles from London when dissension amongst his generals made Charles reluctantly order a retreat. Unknown to them, the capital was virtually undefended, and the Hanoverian King George was about to flee the country.

A few months later a demoralised Jacobite army stopped at Dunblane for the night of 1st February, 1746 before continuing its retreat north. Close behind followed a well-trained Government army of around eight thousand men. It was commanded by the Duke of Cumberland, the third son of George II. At 24 he was the same age as Prince Charles Edward Stuart but was the complete opposite in appearance, being fat, with bovine features and totally lacking in charm. Nevertheless, he was an able general and considerate of his men's welfare — an unusual attribute for those days. But his name is eternally sullied by the grim epithet 'The Butcher' — for the atrocities he ordered after the fatal battle of Culloden Moor. And he is also remembered in the name of a rank Scots weed — 'Stinking Billy'.

His advance guard passed through Dunblane on the

morning of 4th February, leaving word the main army would stop the night there. This news created panic in the town as the people knew everything north of Stirling was thought to be rebellious.

The chief Baillie, James Russell, persuaded the townfolks to forget their differences and go out to welcome the Duke lest he consider the town Highland and raze it to the ground. Baillie Russell stepped forward to greet the Duke and offered him accommodation in his mansion of Allanbank House. He ushered the Duke into the best room but was mortified when the Duke's attendants brought in their own bedding and food, and five sentries were posted outside his door. He was also terrified that his wife — the one who had given Prince Charles the purse of gold — would carry out her threat to knife the Duke as he lay in bed.

There was more mayhem in the streets that night, for the Government army behaved no better than the Jacobite one. One Campbell soldier called at the croft of a devout spinster, and was given broth. He told her that back home in Argyll he simply lifted sheep from the hill whenever he was hungry. The shocked woman scolded him for his sins, and quoted the Bible at him. Donald heard her out patiently and replied, 'Mistress, if you'll ta reat ta Screptur you'll surely reat tere "ta cattles on ta toosan hills are Mine" '. The good woman was so impressed by this argument that she promptly proposed to him, bought him out of the army with her savings, and eloped with him to Argyll!

Most of the Government army was encamped around the baggage carts and artillery in the area south of the present railway station. The bullocks and horses were tethered in the cathedral churchyard under armed guard. This did not prevent the locals from stealing several beasts. During the night one of the sentries accidently discharged his musket, and the ball struck the stone cross on the west gable of the cathedral which remains broken to this day. Local tradition has it that the guard was killed by the falling masonry but that may simply be wishful thinking.

Next morning the bulk of the army marched north in pursuit of the Jacobites. The Duke remained behind to deal with two local men caught looting from a baggage wagon. On learning their names, he exclaimed, 'Brown, is it? A good English name. We have many in the army. Set him free!' Then he turned to the other with a scowl, 'MacNiven! A thieving Highland name — Hang him!' And so the unfortunate MacNiven was the last person to hang from the old public gallows of Dunblane which stood at the junction of the modern Albert Street and the Old Doune Road.

With justice dispensed, the Duke mounted his beautiful grey charger and rode up the street known as the Millrow and into The Cross. He was just passing an ancient mansion belonging to the Strathallan family when in an upstairs window appeared the same serving girl who had polished Prince Charlie's boots five months before. In her hand was a pail of boiling oil which she hurled downwards. The fiery liquid just missed the Duke but struck his horse. The beast reared up in pain and flung the Duke headlong into the muddy street. The girl ran down the stairs and into the underground culvert which carries the Minnie Burn beneath the town, and emerged at its discharge point beside the River Allan to make her escape.

The furious Redcoat soldiers tore several houses apart in their search for her but Dunblane escaped wholesale destruction because the Duke had promised the Archbishop of York he would spare the town. This was for no religious reason — simply that the Archbishop was Robert Drummond, also laird of the neighbouring estate of Cromlix, and owner of most of the property in the town. The badly shaken Duke was helped back onto his horse and eventually followed his army north.

The townsfolk, of all political persuasion, breathed a sigh of relief when both armies had departed. Far to the north, the question of which dynasty was to rule the United Kingdom was settled forever by the crash of cannon and the howl of grapeshot on the sleet-sodden Moor of Culloden.

Allanbank House in Dunblane's Millrow shortly before its demolition in 1963. Here the Duke of Cumberland spent the night of 4th February, 1746, during his pursuit of the Jacobite army of Prince Charles Edward Stuart. Photo: The Royal Commission on the Ancient & Historical Monuments of Scotland.

The serving girl who nearly killed the Duke of Cumberland married a local farmer and lived to a ripe old age. Had her action succeeded, then the history of Britain might have been very different. One story remains. One of the ladies of Dunblane, or it may have been the serving girl, is said to have given birth later to a son by the Prince. The boy was named James Steuart, and later became minister of Anderston Relief Church in Glasgow. He never denied the rumours of his Royal descent, and his congregation presented him with a pulpit beautifully carved with Jacobite roses. He died in 1818, after a ministry there of forty-four years, and was buried in his own churchyard.

His church became known as Anderston Old in 1930, and was demolished in 1966 to make way for the Kingston Bridge which carries the M8 motorway over the River Clyde. His carved pulpit was gifted then to the Free Church in Stornoway. The Kingston Bridge was opened by Her Majesty Queen Elizabeth in 1970. Would she know that just eighty yards from the spot where she performed the opening ceremony lay the mortal remains of one in whose veins may have flowed the blood of the Royal Stewarts?

Modern housing estates now ring Dunblane, for easy motorway access to Glasgow and Edinburgh makes this Perthshire town popular with commuters. The older part of the town would still be recognisable to the ghosts of the Jacobite army. Most of the old cottages looted by the Highlanders still stand although most are now raised a story in height and have slated roofs rather than thatch. Balhaldie House where the Prince met the serving girl still stands although extended in size. Allanbank House, 'Cumberkand's Lodging', fell into decay in recent years and was demolished in 1963. The old mansion known as Strathallan's Lodging, where the serving girl flung down the boiling oil, was pulled down in 1842 to make way for the new County Jail. This was also demolished in 1963 and the site is now a public garden. The estate of Cromlix still remains with the descendants of the Archbishop of York's family. The present owner is the Hon. Ronald Eden, a direct descendant not only of Robert Drummond, Archbishop of York but also of James IV and his secret wife, Margaret Drummond. In 1980 Cromlix House was converted into a luxury country house hotel which in 1983 was voted Best Country House Hotel in Britain.

Jessie, the Flower of Dunblane

Another lady of renown connected with the town was Jessie, the Flower of Dunblane. The ballad of that name was written by Robert Tannahill, the Paisley weaver poet, and first published in the *Scots Magazine* in 1808. The verses were later set to music and it became the most popular ballad in Britain

On the garden on the right was the town house of the Drummonds of Strathallan. From the top window a servant girl flung down a jug of boiling oil at the passing Duke of Cumberland.

throughout most of last century. It was performed delicately in Victorian parlours, sung with gusto in music halls, and bawled out bawdily in coarser drinking houses. Tannahill's works may lack the sheer genius and breadth of imagery of Robert Burns, but 'Jessie, the Flower of Dunblane' deservedly ranks as one of the finest of Scottish love songs.

Tannahill's poems attracted greater attention after his untimely death at the age of 36 in 1810, and then began the search for the girl immortalised in the poem. The mystery of her identity became the great Victorian literary whodunnit, or rather 'who was she', for over sixty years. It was indeed a mystery, for both Tannahill and his friends strongly denied the poem referred to any particular person and insisted that Jessie existed only in the poet's imagination. Yet the poem apparently mentioned details of Dunblane only a resident would have known, although Tannahill had never visited the town himself. In addition, the first few verses are quite different from the rest — as though they had been written some years apart. The poem runs as follows:

The Flower O'Dunblane

The sun has gone down o'er the lofty Ben Lomond,
And left the red clouds to preside o'er the scene.
While lanely I stray, in the calm simmer gloaming
To muse on sweet Jessie, the flower o'Dunblane.

How sweet is the breer, wi its saft faulding blossom!
And sweet is the birk, wi its mantle o green,
Yet sweeter, and fairer, and dear to this bosom,
Is lovely young Jessie, the flower o'Dunblane.

She's modest as any and blithe as she's bonnie;
For guileless simplicity marks her its ain,
And far be the villain, divested of feeling,
Wha'd blight in its bloom the sweet flower o'Dunblane.

Sing on, thou sweet mavis, they hymn to the e'enin,
Thou'rt dear to the echoes of Calderwood glen'
Sae dear to this bosom, sae artless and winnin,
Is charming young Jessie, the flower o'Dunblane.

How lost were my days till I met wi my Jessie!
The sports o the city seemed foolish and vain;
I ne'er saw a nymph I could ca my dear lassie,
Till charmed wi sweet Jessie, the flower o'Dunblane.

Though mine were the station o lofiest grandeur,
Amidst its profusion I'd languish in pain,
And reckon as naething the heicht o its splendour,
If wantin sweet Jessie, the flower o'Dunblane.

It was no uncommon thing for people to go to Dunblane to try and solve the puzzle, and to seek out the real Jessie — and there were many claimants to the title. The guard on the stagecoach between Perth and Stirling in 1821 used to point out a lady of some forty years who then resided in a house adjacent to Kinross's Hotel (now the Stirling Arms). However, as this inn was a changing post for horses, it seems likely this story was invented in order to obtain free drink for the crew on the coach.

A local version named one Jessie Duncan who resided with her father in a still extant row of houses beside the cathedral. The story was that she had fallen in love with a painter working on the rebuilding of nearby Kippenross House, and that he, being a friend of Tannahill's, asked the poet to compose a poem in her honour. Jessie Duncan's grave is still pointed out in the north-west corner of the cathedral churchyard, but she could not have been the heroine because Kippenross House was rebuilt following a fire in 1774, and Tannahill was only born in that year.

A third 'Jessie' featured in a Liverpool magazine of 1829. She was Jessie Monteath, a blue-eyed blonde who had spurned the poet. After the poem became famous, admirers came from all parts to see her, and she eventually eloped with a rake from Edinburgh who installed her in his apartments. She was abandoned by him, and in shame and sorrow drowned herself in the Forth. This might be dismissed simply as the standard Victorian cautionary tale, except that somehow the writer had stumbled on a few clues, but had mixed up the facts. For, despite the poet's denials, there was indeed a real Jessie, and the reason for concealing her identity lay buried in Tannahill's past.

Robert Tannahill was born in a house in Castle Street, Paisley. When he was one, the family moved to a single-storey thatched cottage in Queen Street which his father had built for £60 as a home and workshop for his trade as a handloom weaver. Robert, the fourth son, was a sickly child with a deformed leg, but by the age of six was well enough to begin school. He was an avid reader, and soon began composing impromptu rhymes for the amusement of his classmates. He left school at the age of 12 to be apprenticed

Robert Tannahill (1774—1810), the Paisley weaver-poet.

to his father as a weaver, and his talent for poetry blossomed. Throughout his teens he kept an inkpot and paper attached to his loom to jot down poetic inspiration as it came to him, and he had a battered German flute on which he would capture any old air that caught his fancy.

In 1794 the first popular edition of Robert Burns's 'Tam o Shanter' was published and was particularly well received in Paisley because of its reference to 'her cutty sark o' Paisley harn'. Tannahill read and re-read the poem, and set off to walk the long distance to Alloway to pay homage to the poet. While away, he composed the first of his own poems, 'My ain Kind Dearie'. He was then 20, a mild, slender man of five feet four inches, with a long, aquiline nose, a small mouth with thin lips, and a rounded chin. He also had a chronic, rasping consumptive cough, a pronounced limp, and was desperately shy.

Despite these disabilities, he struck up a friendship in 1795 with Janet, or Jessie, Tennant, who had come from Dunblane with her mother to seek work in the expanding Paisley weaving industry. Tannahill courted Jessie for three years, but not without some difficulty, for Jessie complained to her friends that he was so desperately shy he hardly ever spoke to her. Yet he was deeply in love with Jessie, the only girl he ever went out with, and while courting her secretly wrote the first two verses of his famous poem in her praise.

Jessie did manage to persuade him to accompany her to several small dances at the Masonic Lodge in New Street, but because of his shyness he refused point blank to attend a large ball in 1798. An acquaintance asked if he might take Jessie instead and Tannahill reluctantly agreed. He became stricken with jealousy and hid in the close of Jessie's house to await her return. He was horrified to see Jessie and her escort exchange a quite innocent goodnight kiss, and, biting his knuckles to hide his anguish, he crept silently away.

Tannahill spent the night composing a poem which he took round to Jessie in the morning. He silently handed the manuscript to her and walked away. Poor Jessie glanced at its title of 'Fareweel' and burst into tears when she read the rest:

> Accuse me not, inconstant fair,
>   Of being false to thee,
> For I was true, would still been so,
>   Had'st thou been true to me:
> But when I knew thy plighted lips
>   Once to a rival's prest,
> Love-smother'd independence rose,
>   And spurn'd thee from my breast.
>
> The fairest flow'r in nature's field
>   Conceals the rankling thorn;
> So thou, sweet flow'r! as false as fair,
>   This once kind heart hast torn:
> 'Twas mine to prove the fellest pangs
>   That slighted love can feel;
> 'Tis thine to weep that one rash act,
>   Which bids this long farewell.

F

It was indeed farewell to Jessie, and Tannahill moved to Lancashire in 1800 only to return two years later when his father died. He was now writing poetry seriously and in 1807 published 900 copies of a book of verse. This was eagerly bought by his friends and he made the modest profit of £20. He was now able to complete the remaining verses of 'Jessie, the Flower o'Dunblane', although the new ones lacked the intensity of those written ten years previously. The whole poem was published in the *Scots Magazine* in 1808 and the tune given for the musical accompaniment was 'The Bob o'Dunblane' — a very old ballad to which the Duke of Argyll had referred after the inconclusive battle of Sheriffmuir in 1715. On being informed the Jacobite army was claiming the victory, his Grace quoted, 'Ah weel, if they think it na weel bobbit, we'll bobbit again!'

Tannahill prepared a new version of his poems and sent them to Archibald Constable, the Edinburgh publisher, who returned them unread, although in fairness it was because he was already committed. Tannahill took the rejection personally and felt his talent was finished. He was only 36, but the return of his poems plunged him into depression. He withdrew his entire savings from the bank on 14th May, 1810, and burnt all his manuscripts. His mother found him missing from his bed at 3 a.m., and at 5 a.m. a search party found his body floating in the Caldron Burn. He was buried in an unmarked grave in the West Relief Churchyard, now Castlehead Church, in Canal Street, Paisley.

After his death a friend called R. A. Smith wrote a new tune for 'Jessie' and it became an overnight success. Jessie Tennant, whose goodnight kiss had broken the poet's heart, married her escort of that fateful night and died in Orr Street, Paisley, in 1833, aged 63. Her identity remained a secret until 1874 when her grandchildren in Canada revealed the story which had been passed down the family.

Jessie's birthplace was located in Braeport, Dunblane, where now stands a stone-built cottage with a slightly incorrect inscription above the door: 'Erected 1908. On the site of the cottage where Jessie, The Flower o'Dunblane, was born lived and died'. The bottom four feet of this cottage are original. Nearby is the modern street of Tannahill Terrace, and the outlook from here is over Calderwood Glen and eastwards to Ben Lomond. It was this combination that made many believe Tannahill had visited Dunblane and met Jessie there. In fact, it was the Calderwood Glen near Paisley the poet was referring to and he could easily see the sun go down 'o'er lofty Ben Lomond' from his favourite walk on the Gleniffer Braes.

One final mystery remains. Were both 'Jessie' and 'Fareweel' written not as poems of love and betrayed love but as bitter satire? Subtle clues emerge from both poems. In particular, the word 'flower' was rarely used in literary works of that period because it was common slang for a woman of ill repute. It was partly due to this that 'Jessie' degenerated into a bawdy song amongst the lower classes. Did the embittered Robert Tannahill finally complete 'Jessie, the Flower o'Dunblane' as a final act of revenge for his imagined betrayal? I wonder.

In Praise of Famous Men

The town of Dunblane changed little in size from medieval times until the 1960s when the population was a bare 2500 people. Yet many famous people have been connected with it and many unknown have also left their mark. Amongst the latter was the architect of the Cathedral — anonymous like most such medieval church designers. Tradition says he was returning home after completing his masterpiece when he was murdered at Kinbuck and robbed of all his worldly wealth, which amounted to 1½d. We do not know his name but the artist John Ruskin praised him in a lecture on architecture: 'He was no common man who designed that

Cathedral of Dunblane. I know not anything so perfect in its simplicity, and so beautiful, as far as it reaches, in all the Gothic with which I am acquainted'.

Then there was Timothy Pont whose father was appointed the first protestant minister of the Cathedral in 1561. Timothy later travelled the country to survey it, and about 1600 produced the very first maps of Scotland which were later copied by the famous firm of Blaeu of Amsterdam and incorporated into their *Atlas Novus*. Next is Sir Colin Campbell of Aberuchill who purchased the local estate of Kilbryde in 1669, and whose descendants still reside at Kilbryde Castle. It was Sir Colin, in his role as a Lord of Session, who decided that on strictly legal grounds the delayed Oath of Allegiance of MacDonald of Glencoe should not be presented to the Privy Council. He could not have known his decision would result in the infamous Massacre.

In 1778 a farmer on nearby Glassingall estate called Michael Stirling invented one of the first threshing machines which revolutionised agriculture in Scotland. This estate, once owned by the strongly Jacobite Stewart family, descended through them to two brothers called Alexander and Thomas Smith who inherited it in 1802. They both fell in love with the same girl and she eloped to London with Thomas. She died there giving birth to a son called Thomas. The boy's father drowned in Cuba and young Thomas had the greatest problem proving his identity as there was not a scrap of paper to prove who he was.

He managed to establish contact with his uncle Alexander who provided funds to allow the boy to study art in Rome. Then his uncle died in 1849 without leaving a will and his nephew had enormous difficulty obtaining his rightful inheritance. Robert Louis Stevenson heard this story while holidaying at Bridge of Allan, and from it modelled the plot of his famous novel *Kidnapped*, in which Thomas Smith junior became David Balfour, and his uncle Alexander became Ebenezer Shaw. It will be remembered that all of David Balfour's problems were due to his father and uncle

The small cottage on the extreme left is the original birthplace in Braeport, Dunblane of Jessie Tennant — The Flower o' Dunblane. From a painting of Dunblane c.1800. Photo: The Curators of the Cathedral Museum, Dunblane.

loving the same girl. Thus the real-life 'House of the Shaws' was Old Glassinghall House, a recently restored eighteenth-century laird's house. Thomas Smith junior left funds in his will for the building of the Smith Institute in Stirling, now a flourishing and prize-winning museum and art gallery.

Another literary connection with Dunblane is the probable residence here of the enigmatic author George Douglas Brown who was born in 1869 and who died in mysterious circumstances in 1902. He is believed to have resided with his mother in the house called Elmbank on the Doune Road. In 1900 he wrote the classic and horrific novel *The House with the Green Shutters,* televised in recent years as a play. It seems very likely the fictional town of Barbie was not Ochiltree in Ayrshire, as is supposed, but Dunblane in Perthshire. The House with the Green Shutters is thought to be the house called Strathallan, also on the Doune Road.

James Gillespie Graham, the architect of much of Edinburgh's famed New Town, was born in the Millrow, Dunblane, in 1777. He designed the street facades for Lord Moray, whose land it was, and the developers had to build strictly in accordance with Graham's layout. From this derives the New Town street names of Moray Place, Darnaway Street, and Doune Terrace — the Earl of Moray's son being Lord Doune, and the present holder of that title still lives locally.

During this century other well-known families residing in Dunblane included the Templetons of carpet fame; the Donaldsons of the shipping line of that name; the Burns, also of a well-known shipping line; the Robertsons of the jam firm; also the millionaire John Stewart of the Glasgow steel firm of Stewart and Lloyds who built the mansion of Altwharrie as his private residence. It is now the Royal Scottish Masonic Home.

John, later Lord Reith, lived with his mother for a while in the house called St Ola on the Doune Road. He later became the first Director General of the British Broadcasting Company from 1927 to 1938 and was the virtual creator of the BBC as we know it today. More recently, David Stirling, brother of the late Col. William Stirling of Keir, was the Phantom Major of the Second World War and founder of the Long Range Desert Groups and the SAS Regiment. Keir House, founded by the Stirlings in 1448, and a great deal of the ancestral estates, were sold in recent years to a consortium of Arab businessmen. However, the present laird of Keir, Archibald Stirling, still continues to live locally with his actress wife, Diana Rigg.

CHAPTER 7

From Ardoch to Almondbank

The Roman Fort at Ardoch

The finest and most unusual Roman fort in Britain lies at Ardoch, some ten miles north of Dunblane. Surprisingly, it is neglected and little known, despite being almost perfectly preserved and having a legend of buried treasure.

The fort is part of a huge military complex built around the site of Lindum, one of the five towns of the Damonii tribe, who inhabited most of the country from Perth to Ayr before the Romans arrived.

In 78 A.D. General Gnaeus Julius Agricola assembled an army of 30,000 men at Camelon near Falkirk and marched north to extend the Roman Empire to the very tip of Britain. His army crossed the swamp of the carse of Stirling by means of tree trunks bound together and encamped on the hill to the east of Dunblane. The Roman road north ran parallel to the modern A9 but about a mile nearer the Allan. At Ardoch Agricola threw up a temporary marching camp and before moving on left a cohort of 400 men to begin the construction of a permanent fort.

Agricola's policy was to force the Caledonian tribes back into the mountains by building a series of forts on his route north. Eventually, he brought the combined tribes to battle at Mons Graupius, perhaps in the north-east around Culloden, and killed over 10,000 tribesmen for the loss of 360 legionaries. Agricola was recalled to Rome in 85 A.D. by the Emperor Domitian who was jealous of his success and popularity, and in 90 A.D. the Roman armies withdrew from Scotland.

Eventually the Caledonian tribes regained their strength and began sweeping down into England. To prevent these attacks the Emperor Hadrian built a mighty wall between the Solway and the Tyne. But the attacks continued and in 140 A.D. the British Governor Lollius Urbicus advanced into Scotland. He pushed the Caledonians back and built another great wall of turf and stone which ran for forty miles between the Clyde and Forth. A large and permanent fort was built at Ardoch comprising an inner rampart and two ditches and outer ramparts, and covering some 7.2 acres. This was intended to be an outpost fort while the principal defence and frontier of Roman Britain was the wall of Antonine to the south. Ardoch came under savage attack by the Caledonian tribes, and during excavations here in 1896 clay balls were found inside the perimeter area. The tribesmen heated these and slung them at the thatched roofs of the barrack blocks to set them on fire.

In 158 A.D. the fort was modified by the building of a smaller fort of 5.7 acres inside the existing one. This had the effect of creating five rows of ditches and ramparts, which is very unusual for the overall width of these is about 250 feet, and that is further than a Roman javelin can be thrown. So there is the paradox. Was the country around Ardoch so settled by this time that the defences were unimportant, or was it so dangerous that the ditches were necessary to keep the tribesmen at a distance? The latter seems more likely for Ardoch was finally abandoned in 163 A.D. and in 196 the Romans were forced to withdraw from the Antonine Wall. More and more tribes were rising in revolt and even Hadrian's Wall had to be temporarily evacuated in that year.

In 208 the Emperor Severus invaded Scotland on a punitive expedition and built two huge temporary marching camps outwith the main fort at Ardoch. The larger of these covered 130 acres and the smaller, perhaps for reinforcements, 63 acres. He then made the terrible mistake of trying to push north through the Perthshire Highlands and lost 50,000 men out of 80,000 in the savage wastes. It was a lesson learned, for throughout the centuries no other invader tried to take an

On the east side of the Roman Fort at Ardoch can be seen a defensive causeway running from the east gate to join the Roman road north. In front of the north gate can be seen a ravelin, or javelin throwing platform, and beyond that is the rampart of the earlier fort. The defences on the west side were cut through in the mid-eighteenth century by the construction of the new military road from Stirling to Crieff (now the A822), while those on the south side have been largely obliterated by ploughing. The square outline in the centre of the fort is the foundations of a medieval chapel, long thought to be the site of the Praetorium. The treasure pit lies in this area. Photo: The Royal Commission on the Ancient & Historical Monuments of Scotland.

army north by this route. Severus died in 211 and his son then finally withdrew Roman troops from Scotland and made Hadrian's Wall the boundary of the Empire.

Only a few traces of the five temporary marching camps can still be traced in the fields although aerial photography shows their outlines clearly. The fort, however, is in a remarkable state of preservation. It is sited on a plateau fifty feet above the River Knaik which gave it protection on the west and south faces.

The fort was constructed to a set design devised by Polybius, a military strategist born in B.C. 203. A normal camp built to his plan consisted of an inner rampart and two rows of ditches defending a rectangular area. It was laid out so that each unit knew exactly where it was positioned and could quickly assemble without confusion if under attack. In particular, the expendable auxiliary troops were usually quartered around the perimeter to protect the Roman legions. The veteran legions were based around the praetorium, or general's quarters, in the middle of the camp, in case of mutiny. Ardoch measures 500 feet by 420 feet and under the Polybian system could hold 1200 men and in its final form contained stone barrack blocks set out in exact rows. The fortifications on the east side are almost completely intact. The inner rampart rises eighteen feet from the foot of the ditch in front and originally consisted of a stone wall backed by earth. The east gate is also clearly seen and originally would have had a stone and wood gate and watchtower. From here the causeway runs out to join the Roman road north and at the last ditch takes a clever twist to give additional protection. The ditches and ramparts were cleared of undergrowth a few years ago and virtually follow their original profile and depth.

The south-side defences are now almost removed by ploughing while those on the west side have been cut away by the building of the Stirling to Crieff military road of General Wade in 1724. The north side shows the peculiar cutting off the earlier fort and another causeway running out into the annexe camp. This latter held about 4000 men. Another point of interest is the unusual and ingenious way the Roman engineers stopped off the middle ditch of the north side at the north-east and west corners.

The interior of the fort is now a flat, grassy area with the stone foundations of a small building visible in the middle. For many years it was thought this marked the praetorium, even by such distinguished antiquaries and surveyors as Sir Robert Sibbald, George Chalmers, and General Roy, although its site did not conform to a standard Roman layout. However, the excavations carried out in 1896 by the Society of Antiquaries proved this was the remains of a medieval chapel enclosed by a wall and apparently surrounded by a small burial ground. Although not mentioned in any ecclesiastical history, an old document showed the chapel belonged to the Priory of Inchmahome and was known as the Chapel Raith, or Church of the Fort.

After the Romans abandoned Ardoch it disappeared into the Dark Ages. The first mention of the fort in more modern times is in a letter written by James, Lord Drummond, later 4th Earl of Perth, to his kinsman Patrick Drummond, on January 15, 1672. Adapted into modern English, it reads:

'My dearest friend, — Towards the forest belonging to my father two countrymen were building a corn kiln on the foundations of an old one.

'They found a great ring of gold and a considerable amount of money which they sold to pedlars for a handful of common coin . . . who carried it to Perth and sold it to goldsmiths . . . the silver was so good that it would not mix until a third of alloy had been joined to them.

'They say there was more than a bushel of them; but all the inquiry I could make could not get me any of them.

'The leaguer [laager] of the Romans lay for one whole winter at Ardoch, some four miles or more from that place, and there is to be seen there entrenchments and fortifications in circular lines deeper in some places than that a man on horseback can be seen: and north-east from that are more trenches, alike in form and largeness: but the ground being much better has made the people, against my grandfather's orders, till them down in places.

'There was near there a round opening like the mouth of a narrow well, of a great depth, into which my grandfather ordered a malefactor to go, who (glad of the opportunity to escape hanging) went and brought up a spur and buckle of brass; which were lost the time a garrison of Oliver's [Cromwell] disposessed us of Drummond [Castle].

'There was found there a stone upon which was cut an inscription to show that a captain of the Spanish Legion died there. If you please, I shall copy it for you. It is rudely cut.'

The stone mentioned is now in the Hunterian Museum of Glasgow University and, translated, it reads: 'To the Shade of Ammonius Damion, Centurion of the First Cohort of the Spanish Stipendiaries, who served for Twenty Seven Years, his Heirs have erected this monument'.

The unfortunate criminal who obtained the stone was sent down again but expired in the foul air.

In 1690 another condemned man was obtained — this was in the days before the abolition of Barony Courts in 1748 — and he also was offered the choice of hanging or descending the pit. He chose the latter, and was lowered on a rope. He brought up spears and helmets, and reported seeing piles of gold and silver objects at a greater depth.

He was promptly sent down again, but he, too, died before managing to obtain any more objects. After this no more attempts were made. The articles recovered lay at Ardoch House until carried off by some looting soldiers of Argyll's army after the Battle of Sherrifmuir in 1715.

Sir Robert Sibbald, family physician to the Perth family, carried out a careful examination of the camp in 1695, and published his findings in his *Scotia Antiqua*. Although his ground plan is inaccurate, it is interesting to note that he states that below the camp 'there are caves or vaults'.

One hundred years later the Rev. John Scott wrote in the *Old Statistical Account* of Scotland (Muthill Parish) of 1795:

'That there was a subterranean passage from the smaller one [camp] under the bed of the river is more than probable . . .

'There was a hole near the side of the Praetorium that went in a sloping direction for many fathoms in which, it was generally believed, treasures as well as Roman antiquities might be found.'

He then advances some novel theories as to how the foul air might be dealt with, including putting down heaps of burning grass to fumigate the shaft!

But long before any of these writers there was an old rhyme which, according to the *History of Scottish Rhymes*, goes back to time immemorial without any significant alteration. It runs:

> Between the Roman camp at Ardoch,
> And the Grainin Hill of Kier,
> Lies seven Kings' ransoms,
> For seven hundred years.

The Grainin' (Sunny) Hill of Kier is a wooded hillock about a quarter mile to the south-west of the main camp, behind the village of Braco, and it was a strongly fortified Roman outpost. The visible extensive terracing indicates it had also been a hill fort of the Caledonians.

The hill was rumoured to be connected to the main camp by a subterranean tunnel. It was not unknown for the Romans to link forts by means of a sunken, covered passage. Other opinions suggest the tunnel might have been either an underground store, or it may have led under the bed of the river to collect filtered water.

Certainly, during the excavations of 1896, one or two pits of seven- or eight-foot diameter were uncovered near the centre of the camp. These were found to go down a great way, but they were not explored because of the cost of shoring the sides, and excavating the silted-up shafts.

Unfortunately, the exact location of the treasure pit is no longer known, although an early writer describes it as being seven paces east of the supposed praetorium. It was covered over in 1720 during the forty years which Sir William Stirling of Ardoch spent in Russia, serving in the Czar's army.

An old man, who was the tenant of Ardoch House, lost a

Memorial stone to Ammonius Damion, Centurion of the Spanish Stipendiaries, recovered from the Ardoch treasure pit and now in the Hunterian Museum of Glasgow University.

favourite dog down the hole while he was hunting hares. He ordered a millstone to be placed across the mouth, and subsequent ploughing removed all traces of the spot, although a careful search was made at a later date.

The legend of the lost Roman treasure is not too improbable, for there are many indications that Ardoch was evacuated in a hurry, and possibly valuables were hidden in expectation of being recovered when reinforcements arrived. But, of course, the legions were not to know that they were being withdrawn for good.

A more modern item of interest is the remains of a stone entrance gate set into the wall beside the modern highway. In 1842 it was known that Queen Victoria would pass by the fort after staying at Drummond Castle. The landowner, Colonel Moray Stirling of Ardoch House, made an entrance into it and erected two stone pillars connected by an arch. This bore the initials V and A, and a wrought-iron gate was fitted. Unfortunately, the Queen did not feel like leaving her carriage, but a contemporary report says Prince Albert expressed great interest and made a careful examination of the whole complex. The pillars and arch survived until the 1930s when they began to crumble. The arch was then lowered and built into the lower wall.

Today, as one stands upon the ramparts, it is not difficult to imagine the scenes of nearly 2000 years ago, when the Romans first threw up these mighty earthworks and advanced north for the glory of Rome.

The outlook over the empty, desolate moors is virtually unchanged since the foreign soldiers stamped their feet in the cold and gazed nervously northwards to the black, forbidding mountains where the tribes were gathering for yet another attack.

There is one final strange tale of Ardoch Roman Fort. A few years ago photographs were taken of a ruined farmhouse near the camp which was being renovated. It is a curious fact that when these were developed the form of a Roman legionary appeared in every one.

But I too had a peculiar experience a few years ago which I still cannot explain rationally.

In 1974 I lived on a new housing estate on a hill above Dunblane. I was working late one September night when I went outside for some fresh air. It was a clear frosty night with not a sound to be heard anywhere.

As I turned to go back indoors, I suddenly heard a strange noise coming across the fields to the south. It sounded like a large number of people on the move with faint voices rising and falling. I listened in puzzlement, then decided my imagination was playing tricks and went inside. But I couldn't get the curious matter off my mind and twenty minutes later I went outside again.

The noise was now much louder and was now passing immediately behind the houses on the other side of the street. For the first time in my life I felt the skin rise from my scalp and my hair bristle. I could now almost make out individual voices but couldn't understand what they were saying. But quite clearly I was sure I heard the tramp of marching feet and the jingle of what sounded like weapons and armour.

The noise went on and on until I turned inside and went straight to bed. I was convinced I had been overworking and put the experience from my mind until a week later when I called on an elderly couple who had moved in further up the street. I was talking to them when their dog rose up to stretch. 'Sit down!' its mistress commanded. 'You're seeing things again.'

'What things?' I asked.

'Well, the strangest thing happened last week,' she replied. 'We were sitting up reading about 1.00 a.m. when the cat and dog suddenly woke up. They stood bolt upright with all their hair bristling up their backs and seemed to watch something crossing the lounge for about twenty minutes. They were terrified.'

When I questioned them further, I was astonished to learn this strange episode had taken place on the same night and at precisely the same time I had heard the invisible army pass by. I knew from my researching that the housing estate was built on the site of two large Roman marching camps. I located some old aerial photographs which clearly showed the outlines of the camps. They also showed the line of the Roman road which ran north directly behind the houses on the other side of my street.

I also began to study the paranormal. I found that some modern researchers speculate that 'ghosts' are not literally spirits of the dead but are formed by a strong emotional or violent event which registers itself in the earth's magnetic field — a bit like a magnetic video recording. For some reason this can be picked up by receptive persons at particular times. This was an idea I felt I could accept. But what event had been so terrible that its occurrence on that Roman road had been recorded for eternity?

Well, in A.D. 117 the Caledonian tribes in Scotland rose in revolt and destroyed the small Roman garrisons. The

The gate let into the wall for the visit to Ardoch Fort by Queen Victoria and Prince Albert in 1842.

Emperor Hadrian ordered the elite IX Hispana Legion, stationed at York, to march north to subdue the tribes. This unit had been known as the Unlucky Ninth ever since A.D. 60 when it had flogged Queen Boadicea of the south of England Iceni tribe and raped her daughters. Boadicea had cursed the legion to eternity and it was cut to pieces when she led all the tribes in a bloody revolt.

The IX Legion was re-formed but never prospered. However, it was still an elite unit of 4000 battle-hardened legionnaires when it marched into Scotland in the autumn of 117 A.D., and from there it disappeared from the face of the earth. Not a trace of the finest fighting unit in the Roman army has ever been found — not a body, not a coin, not a weapon. Four thousand soldiers simply vanished into the mist.

I never heard the noise again and I later moved to another part of Dunblane. I had forgotten all about the incident until October 1984 when I was giving a lecture on local history to a ladies' club. One of the members came up afterwards to say how interested she had been. 'I never knew the Romans came as far north as this,' she said. Then she astounded me by adding with a laugh, 'I wonder if that was the ghost of a Roman army I heard.'

When I asked her what she meant, she said she had moved into a house on the other side of the street from my old property. 'You won't believe this,' she said, 'but I was putting the cat out one night when I heard what sounded like an army passing right through my back garden. It was fascinating but when I told my family they just laughed.' It turned out that she had heard this at 1.00 a.m. on exactly the same date in September that I had heard the sound ten years earlier.

So what exactly did I hear? Was it all imagination or coincidence or did I hear the doomed Ninth Legion marching to its terrible unknown fate nearly 2000 years ago?

The Suicides' Graveyard

The modern A822 road follows the line of the old military road until a mile past Ardoch Fort where it swings to the right. The old road continues straight ahead and up the hill, passing a recent forestry plantation on the summit. In the centre of this wood is a ¼-acre of unplanted moorland, left untouched because this was a suicides' graveyard. It lay on the boundary of the parishes of Ardoch and Muthill, and because suicides were not allowed to be buried in consecrated ground, the unfortunates were brought up here. The Forestry Commission discovered the unhallowed burial ground from old maps and decided it should be kept clear of trees. The passage of time has caused the graves to sink and the numerous depressions give an indication of how many must have been interred here.

The Scottish Empress of Morocco

The road carries on and descends to the Machany Water which it crosses by a delightful stone bridge built by General Wade's engineers. Here lived Helen Gloag, a simple country girl who attained the exalted rank of Empress of Morocco through no desire or effort on her part.

She was born in January, 1750, at Wester Pett near Muthill, the daughter of Andrew Gloag and Ann Key. In that year, the surrounding district lay subdued and poverty-stricken, for its principal landowner, the Earl of Perth, had been attainted for his part in the '45 Jacobite Uprising, and his Drummond Castle estate had been forfeited to the Crown. As the Episcopal religion was still banned, Helen Gloag was baptised secretly in St. James's Church, Muthill, on 14th February, 1750.

Some time later, her family moved a short distance to the Mill of Steps on the Machany Water where her father was in business as a blacksmith. This little hamlet consisted then of a waulk mill, a smithy, and a square of cottages beside the small stone bridge which carried the recently-built Stirling to Crieff military road over the river.

Helen grew up to be a striking beauty, with green eyes, golden red hair and high cheekbones set in a pale, oval face. Her mother died when she was quite young, and her father re-married, but unfortunately the new Mrs. Gloag and her growing stepdaughter did not get on together. Matters became worse when Helen was in her teens, for she began a friendship with a local farmer, John Byrne, who was eleven years her senior. She made frequent visits to his nearby farm of Lurg to play cards, and although it was quite an innocent relationship, it became the source of ever-increasing friction with her stepmother.

When Helen was 19, she decided she could stand it no longer, and she resolved to emigrate to South Carolina in America along with several of her girl friends. The little party made its way to Greenock in May, 1769, and took passage on a ship which they hoped would carry them to a new and better life.

The vessel had been at sea for only a few weeks when from the masthead came the dreaded cry, 'Corsairs!' — and bearing in fast on all sides came a pack of the feared xebecs. These swift, three-masted ships of 200 tons carried 20 guns and 200 of the terrible Salle pirates. The scourge of the seas, these men had their base at the Moroccan port of Salle where a sand bar at the harbour mouth allowed the nimble xebecs to sail across to safety, leaving any larger pursuer floundering impotently outside.

Salle, an ancient walled town, had become notorious for its school of pilots and piracy, founded originally by Moors driven from Spain. Its graduates roamed the seas as far north as Orkney seeking booty and slaves. In 1631, they had raided a village in the west of Ireland, and carried off 250 people. Raids by the pirates were common all around the British coast.

Some of the pirates were renegades — captured Europeans who had spurned Christianity to escape slavery, and had sworn allegiance to the Sultan of Morocco and embraced Mohammedanism. Many Scots were amongst them, including one Robert Carr who changed his name to Omar, and was given command of a 16-gun zebec in 1757. The Sultan of Morocco owned over half the pirate fleet, and collected a tax of 60% on all captured goods.

The defenceless merchant ship carrying Helen and her friends was no match for the well-armed pirate vessels, and the savage corsairs swarmed aboard cutting down all who resisted. The male survivors were chained and sent into the galleys as slaves, while the women were herded into the hold under guard. The triumphant pirates made their way back to Salle with their prize, and as the terrified women were brought up on deck they gazed in horror at scenes of utter barbarism, for around Salle's walls were fixed human heads (this custom was last recorded in 1912 when forty rebel heads adorned the walls of Fez, and the Salle pirates were not finally stamped out till 1921).

The country the girls were entering was a living hell for captured Europeans, as Moroccans regarded Christians as sub-human, and of less worth than animals. However, by 1769, conditions had improved somewhat since the reign of the terrible Mulai (Prince) Ismail, who had ruled Morocco with a bloodstained iron fist from 1672 to 1727. Mulai Ismail was of part-Negro descent, and delighted in matching the fairest of his captives with the blackest of his Negro bodyguard.

During his reign, over 25,000 Christian slaves were employed in huge construction works, particularly the palace at Meknes whose stables alone stretch for three miles, and were designed to hold 12,000 horses. The slaves were kept at night in underground dungeons, and treated with the utmost cruelty. During his tours of inspection, Mulai Ismail would suddenly order a slave to be flung alive into a lime kiln, or impaled on a stake, while his favourite delight was to saw a man in half from the head down. His cruelty extended to his own people, and he would lop off an attendant's head to test the sharpness of his sword.

He had a harem of 2000 women, each of whom he visited only once, and had 1000 children of whom only 520 sons survived, for he had his daughters strangled at birth.

Helen and her friends were shipped ashore to be spat at and reviled by the onlookers. The men were led away in chains to an unimaginable living death, while the less attractive women were taken out and given to the Moorish soldiers for their amusement. Those of better looks, including Helen, were dragged to the slave market to be exhibited for sale. Here, Helen's beauty attracted the

On the east side of General Wade's military road and bridge over the Machany Water, near Muthill, can be traced the foundations of the Mill of Steps where lived Helen Gloag, Empress of Morocco.

attention of an astute merchant who paid a large sum for her and then presented her to the Grand Vizier ibn Abdullah, the ruler of Morocco.

He had inherited the throne in 1757, and was more enlightened than his fearful grandfather although he still encouraged slavery and piracy. He quickly became infatuated by his new concubine, and shortly after, he made Helen his fourth wife and raised her to the rank of Empress. This must have been not long after Helen arrived, for in 1769 an Englishwoman called Mrs. Crisp was captured while travelling in Minorca, and taken into the Sultan's harem. Inexplicably, she was freed unharmed soon after, and wrote a book about her adventures, *The Female Captive*. In it she recorded that she had heard of the Sultan having an 'Irish' wife and wondered if it was because of her that she had been released.

Unfortunately, Morocco was a closed country for centuries, and the very few native records that were written would not consider mentioning anything so unimportant as a woman — even if she was an Empress. However, there are one or two fragments to be gleaned from the writings of the few Europeans who were allowed to enter the country. Perhaps it was due to Helen's influence that an English doctor, William Lempriere, was allowed into Morocco in 1789, and even permitted to examine the ladies in the harem.

He wrote later that while he had met three of the royal wives, the fourth was in the town of Fez, but rumour had it she was English. This seems to fit, for Helen would then have been 39, and after 30, a Sultana was usually sent into exile with her children.

There seems little doubt that Helen did exert a strong influence over her husband, for later in his reign the shipping of negro slaves from Morocco (by the English!) was forbidden. British captives were released unharmed, slavery dwindled away, and even the Salle pirates were officially abolished. Most interestingly, trade compacts and treaties were entered into with the British, and in 1782, aid was given to them in their battle for Gibraltar. Thus it seems more than likely that it was due partly to Helen Gloag that Gibraltar is British today.

The Sultan Mohammed began to build towns for trading purposes, and his new Atlantic port of Mogador (now Essaoira) attracted traders from all over Europe. Here came vast camel caravans from the interior, laden with ivory, gold, carpets and wax. The port of Mogador was originally named after its patron saint, Sidi Magdoul, whose shrine still stands. Believe it or not, Sidi Magdoul is said to have been a Scots seaman called John MacDougall, but when he was there, and what made him a Muslim saint, is unknown.

Helen had two sons by the Sultan, and seems to have become reconciled to her strange life in a barbarous land. She wrote home frequently, and sent many gifts of Moroccan craftsmanship not only to her family, but also to her friend

John Byrne. These were conveyed by Robert Gloag, Helen's sea-captain brother who made many trips to see her, and it is likely he was one of several Scots who were permitted to establish trading houses.

In 1790, Sultan Mohammed ibn Abdullah died, and as Helen's sons were too young to rule, he had nominated a nephew to succeed him. Unfortunately, his disowned son by a German concubine, the half-mad, red-haired Mulai Yazeed, raised a revolt and grabbed his father's throne. The first act of the sadistic Yazeed was to roast alive his father's faithful Vizier, and then to throw his harem into the streets. After the Basha of Tangier held out against him, Yazeed ordered the man's aged mother to be put to death in a horrific manner. The details of his mindless cruelty are not for these pages.

To escape Yazeed's reign of terror, Helen sent her sons, then aged about 21 and 16, to the town of Teuten, where they sought sanctuary in one of the few newly-permitted Christian monasteries. She then appealed for help to the British Government, claiming her British citizenship, and a fleet prepared to sail to her assistance from Gibraltar. An officer, Lt. Colonel Jardine, was sent ahead to ascertain the situation, but before he arrived, Yazeed's troops probably overran the monastery and murdered the two princes. Politics being what they are, the fleet sent to help Helen was then directed to aid the usurper Yazeed in his bid to throw the Spanish out of the Moroccan town of Ceuta. For the next two years, Morocco once again became a living nightmare until Yazeed died of a wound in 1792.

Unfortunately, Helen's fate is unknown, but it is possible that she survived Yazeed's reign. Some years ago, two ladies from Muthill were visiting the modern town of Rabat built on the other bank of the river from the old pirate town of Salle, and now the Moroccan capital, when their guide suddenly pointed out a monument which he said had been erected to the memory of a Scottish Empress. Morocco still seems to be something of a closed country, for despite many enquiries I have been unable to track down the memorial's location.

Helen's sea-captain brother retired to the old family cottage at Mill of Steps and died there in 1830 aged 77. Many of her letters and gifts were in the possession of a Mrs. McCall, granddaughter of the farmer John Byrne, until her death in 1922 aged 83. Mrs. McCall also owned the chair in which Helen had sat to play cards at Lurg farm when she was a teenager, and this was rescued from a rubbish pile after a disposal sale. It was known as the Empress Chair, but unfortunately only a few worm-eaten parts survive today in Muthill.

The hamlet of Mill of Steps has now vanished apart from stone foundations, but there is still a living reminder of the Scottish Empress of Morocco. In Muthill today lives Mrs. Joyce Turnbull, a descendant of Helen Gloag's brother who has the same high cheekbones, green eyes, and the auburn hair — known as the Gloag Hair — which so attracted the Sultan Mohammed that he made this country girl into his Empress.

Bessie Bell and Mary Gray

A few miles to the north two other country girls achieved immortality through their tragic death and became renowned through the old ballad called 'Twa Bonnie Lasses':

> O Bessie Bell an' Mary Gray!
>   They were twa bonnie lasses,
> They biggit a bower on yon burn-brae,
>   An' theekit it owre wi' rashes.
>
> They theekit it owre wi' rashes green.
>   They happit it roun' wi' heather;
> But the pest cam' frae the Burrows-toun
>   An' slew them baith thegither.

H

The plague! — the very mention of that word used to strike terror into the people of Scotland. Six major outbreaks of the dreaded disease occurred between the fourteenth and seventeenth centuries. The first, the Black Death, broke out in 1349 and killed twenty-five million people in Europe. Nine-tenths of the population of England perished, and one third in Scotland, in all a total of 800,000 people, leaving the two countries deserted wastelands.

The last visitation of the plague, in 1645, was by far the worst. It was probably imported from the continent by mercenary soldiers fighting in the English Civil War, and the disease was spread rapidly by the movement of armies.

The plague crossed the Border in April 1645, when the first outbreak occurred in the town of Kelso. The houses of the infected were set on fire, but the flames went out of control and destroyed the town. The disease then spread slowly north. When it reached Edinburgh in June 1645, Parliament transferred swiftly to Stirling. The disease followed rapidly, leaping from town to town, and even today it is possible to track its progress from old maps and local traditions. At Dunblane Cathedral, a quarter of the churchyard is devoid of gravestones. This is said to be the local plague pit which none dare open in later years for fear of releasing the disease.

When the plague arrived in Stirling, Parliament moved to Perth on 24th July 1645. A Covenanting army arrived here about the same time and was besieged by Montrose's Highland army. Both armies departed at the beginning of August, but they left the plague behind. The first victims were reported on 4th August, and Parliament was hastily adjourned. Then the disease struck Perth with ferocity. The terrified inhabitants prevented the burial of the dead in hallowed ground, and the parish church was closed from 22nd August 1645 until 3rd January 1646. That was in the early stages before the living were driven in panic from the streets.

Most of the population fled into the surrounding

The plague entered Scotland in April 1645 and spread rapidly north. An open area in Dunblane Cathedral churchyard, unmarked by graves, is said to have been the local plague pit.

countryside, particularly to the parish of Rhynd, where they lived in huts. As panic mounted, families were abandoned by their relatives, and the scene in Perth became a nightmare. Nearly 3000 were to die, and corpses lay rotting in the streets.

The parish of Moneydie, a few miles west of Perth, was initially unaffected. Here stood the estate of Lynedoch whose laird was Patrick Gray, and whose seat was a castle on the banks of the Almond. He had a beautiful daughter called Mary Gray, aged about 20, whose lifelong friend was her cousin Bessie Bell. Bessie had been visiting Lynedoch when news came that the plague was spreading into the countryside. It was decided that both girls should retreat to a secluded spot about a mile to the west, near the Almond. Here, at a place called Burnbraes, beside the Brauchie Burn, they built a little hut of wattle, roofed with rushes and floored with heather. They lived happily for a time in their solitude, surrounded by the creatures of the wood. Then their food ran out and the girls were forced to seek out and eat black snails, to avoid starvation.

Bessie Bell had a lover who could not bear the separation, and made a secret visit to the little bower in the woods. At first, the girls were displeased because of the risk of infection, but they soon forgave him. The youth was horrified to learn their diet consisted of snails, and he came back several times with food. On his last trip he encountered a travelling pedlar who, tradition says, was a Jew. The pedlar showed the youth a fine, lace handkerchief, though some say it was a string of pearls. The love-struck lad eagerly bought it as a gift for his beloved Bessie, and when she put it on, her cousin Mary clapped her hands in admiration.

Alas, only a few hours later, Bessie fell sick with the symptoms of the plague. Mary nursed her gently, tending her until she, too, was struck down. Then the two girls lay clasped together in their hut until death mercifully came upon them. It was said later that the pedlar had passed through Perth and had stolen Bessie's gift from the body of a plague victim lying in the street.

Bessie's lover found the girls' bodies when he returned a few days later and he ran to Mary's father with the awful news. As no one dared touch them it is likely the few immune local people who were forced to become 'cleansers' were sent to the spot. They carried the bodies a few hundred yards to the ford over the Almond at the Dronach (sorrowful) Haugh with the intention of carrying them to the Gray family burial vault at Methven Collegiate Church. However, when the party reached the ford they were prevented from crossing by the people of Methven who refused to allow plague victims to be buried in their churchyard. It appears the 'cleansers' simply left the bodies lying on the ground, for the old ballad tells that the girls 'maun lie in Dronach Haugh and beik [bake] fornent the sun'. The remains were apparently interred much later, probably after the plague had subsided, and a cairn of stones was placed on top.

After the plague died out around 1647, the story of Bessie

Bell and Mary Gray was immortalised by an unknown balladmaker, and became known throughout Scotland.

The poet Allan Ramsay (1686–1758) adapted the ballad into a new song of his own which was published in 1721. The story was well-known by 1737 when Major George Augustus Barry of the 50th Regiment purchased the estate of Lynedoch. Years later, in 1781, he wrote to the Society of Antiquaries in Scotland: 'I was shown (in part of my ground called the Dronach Haugh) a heap of stones, almost covered with briers, thorns and ferns, which they assured me was the burial place of Bessie Bell and Mary Gray. I removed all the rubbish from this little classic ground, enclosed it with a wall, planted it round with flowering shrubs, made up the grave double, and fixed a stone in the wall, on which were engraved the names of Bessie Bell and Mary Gray'.

Robert Burns was invited to view the spot while travelling to Blair Atholl in 1787, but did not stop, and so the story remained untouched by his hand. A noted traveller of the period, the Hon. Mrs. Murray of Kensington, visited the site in 1799 and recorded: 'I plainly saw the marks of two graves by the rising of the soil. The third, that of the lover, said to be at the foot, I could not find'. The 'rising of the soil' was due to Major Barry's having heaped up two mounds some sixty-two years before.

The burial place had also undergone some alteration after the Lynedoch estate was purchased in 1787 by Thomas Graham of Balgowan, later General Graham.

After acquiring the estate, Graham saw that the wall around Bessie Bell and Mary Gray's burial place had fallen down. He replaced it with ornamental iron railings, planted yew trees around, and placed a large stone over the graves inscribed with the words. 'They Lived – They Loved – They Died'.

This bluff military approach did not find favour with a Mrs. Ogilvie who condemned it in verse in her *Highland Minstrelsy*:

> We seek but freedom — from us far
> Be tablet-stone and iron bar,
>   Our peaceful ashes crushing;
> Let us again feel sun and showers,
> And hear the tinkle of the flowers,
>   And Almond's waters gushing.

Numerous other poets composed verse, both good and bad, around the story. John Leyden (1775–1811), who assisted Sir Walter Scott with his *Border Minstrelsy*, transferred the scene of the tragedy to the Borders in his 'Scenes of Infancy'. The original ballad air was used by John Gay for the duet in Act III, Scene 8 of his famous *Beggar's Opera* which begins:

> A curse attends that woman's love
> Who always would be pleasing.

James Duff, a Logiealmond gardener-poet of the early nineteenth century, also wrote a rambling poem based on the original ballad. This is of little value except that Duff was the only person who accurately described Bessie Bell as the niece of Mary Gray's father. All other sources state incorrectly that Bessie was the daughter of the Laird of Kinvaid although no one of that name ever possessed that estate.

I had thought the Rev. William Hetherington had written the final epitaph to Bessie Bell and Mary Gray in his *Dramatic Sketches:* 'That long deserted bower, and those twin graves, Shall they be all forgot? Shall future times of them know nothing?'

I had assumed the answer to that to be in the affirmative, and that only a few of the older generation would remember the ballad. However, when I went in search of the spot, I was told by Sandy Brown, gamekeeper on Lord Mansfield's Lynedoch estate, that many people still come from all parts to visit the girls' grave. Following his directions, I found the railed-off burial place on the now wooded Dronach Haugh.

A lonely railed-off grave on the Dronach Haugh marks the resting place of Bessie Bell and Mary Gray. Bessie's lover is said to be buried at her feet. Beneath the soil lies the stone inscribed 'They Lived — They Loved — They Died'.

Alas, it once again lies neglected and dilapidated, and the stone which General Graham placed upon the graves has sunk beneath the soil. Overhead stands one of the yew trees which he planted.

A few hundred yards away is the Brauchie Burn, and beside it I found the outlines of a building measuring four yards square — all that remains of the little hut in the woods where Bessie Bell and Mary Gray 'lived, loved and died' during that terrible period in Scottish history.

But the names of the two friends are not forgotten today. Scots immigrants to Ulster in the seventeenth century took the ballad with them and used it to re-name topographical features. Thus the twin hills of 'Bessie Bell' (1300 feet) and 'Mary Gray' (800 feet) face each other on either side of the Northern Ireland A5 road Newton Stewart, Co. Tyrone. A century or so later, and the descendants of these Ulster Scots began to migrate to America around 1730. They also took with them the ballad of the girls. These immigrants moved to the area west of the Virginian mountains where religious freedom was allowed, and settled in the Shenandoah valley. Someone noticed two hills which bore a close resemblance to those at home and so today the hills of 'Betsy Bell' and 'Mary Gray' dominate the town of Staunton, Virginia.

CHAPTER 8

In the Heart of Strathearn

Tullibardine Castle, now long vanished, was the first seat in Perthshire of the Murrays descended from a Fleming called Freskin who came to Scotland in the time of David I. He was given land in Morayshire whence he took the name de Moravia, later to become Murray and Moray. A century later, his descendant married Adda, daughter of the Celtic Seneschal of Strathearn, and thus the Murrays acquired the lands of Tullibardine, near Auchterarder.

In the fifteenth century the then laird married the daughter of Sir John Colquhoun of Luss, and they had seventeen sons. These sons are the progenitors of the many Murray families scattered across Scotland. On one occasion Sir William took his sons to visit Stirling Castle at a time when James V was trying to curtail the arrogance of his nobles and had just passed a law forbidding anyone to travel with more than one retainer. The king was furious to learn that Sir William Murray of Tullibardine was approaching Stirling with an armed 'tail' of no less than thirty-seven men, and had Sir William dragged into his presence. James angrily demanded an explanation, and in reply the laird ushered in his sons, and meekly said that he had brought his children to see the king, and surely his Majesty would allow them a servant each? The king laughed loudly, and welcomed Sir William and his sons to court.

A later Sir William was appointed joint keeper of Stirling Castle, and guardian of the young James VI. He was exiled for breaking the Earl of Argyle's face with the hilt of his sword — an action which many considered long overdue. However, during his absence there was great difficulty in collecting the king's cattle taxes, and there was no one strong enough to enforce the law. In frustration, the king cried out

The pre-Reformation Chapel of the Holy Trinity at Tullibardine
was founded in 1446 by Sir David Murray, Bailiff of Strathearn.
Tullibardine Castle, now vanished, lay a half mile to the north.

that if only he had Will Murray back, then his dues would be
collected. This sign of forgiveness was quickly relayed, and
Sir William returned to be made Lord Comptroller. His son,
John, was made Master of the Household and a Privy
Councillor, and was raised to the peerage in 1606 as 1st Earl
of Tullibardine.

The 2nd Earl married the only daughter of the Stewart
Earl of Atholl, and the son of this marriage was confirmed as
the first of a new line in the Atholl Earldom. A later
descendant was created Duke of Atholl and, ever since, the
heir to that title has been known as the Marquis of
Tullibardine. The surname Stewart was adopted at the time
of elevation, and although the Duke could call out almost
3000 men at the '45 Uprising, it was only as feudal retainers
and not as clansmen. Indeed, it was not till 1958 that the
Duke of Atholl dropped the name of Stewart, and was

recognised as Chief of Clan Murray, and all its septs. Whether Stewarts or Murrays, they were strong Jacobites, and the Marquis of Tullibardine was attainted in 1715. His talented brother, Lord George Murray, played a prominent role in the '45, and had the Prince's campaign been left to him, then it is probable Charles Edward Stuart would have been restored to his rightful throne.

The Tullibardine family also owned the Isle of Man, until sold to the British Government in 1765 for £60,000 and an annuity of £2,000.

Tullibardine Castle, the ancestral home of this fascinating family, saw little fighting throughout the centuries. It was visited by several monarchs, surrendered to the Duke of Argyll in 1715, was lived in by Lord George Murray, and was pulled down in 1830 to provide stones for local farm buildings.

Tullibardine and the *Great Michael*

Near the Castle, and still surviving, is one of the few pre-Reformation churches to have escaped the over-zealous hands of the sixteenth-century Reformers, and is still in perfect condition. It was built in 1446 by Sir David Murray in the traditional cruciform shape, and was the burial place of the Murrays of Tullibardine until they moved to Blair Castle.

Later it became the interment vault for the Earls of Perth whose estate lay immediately to the north. Various coffins can still be seen beneath the gratings, and a small one contains the arm of a Viscount Strathallan who lost it in a threshing machine. Philosophically, he had it placed in the small box and interred amidst full honours with the remark that it could wait until the rest of him joined it later! Today the chapel is in the care of the Department of the Environment, and is an excellent example of an early collegiate church.

But at the site of the old Castle there is nothing to be seen, neither rubble nor foundations. However, I did locate the only known print of it in the National Library of Scotland, and while researching I found volumes on the Murrays, and on a page in the last book I noticed that some earlier reader had written the word 'Pitscottie' beside a reference to Tullibardine Castle.

Robert Lindsay of Pitscottie in Fife was a garrulous sixteenth-century diarist, and Scotland's first popular historian. I obtained a copy of his *Historie and Chronicles of Scotland*, written in 1570, and thumbed through it until I came to his account of the reign of James IV, that restless, inventive and romantic monarch who combined every trait, good and bad, of the Stuart dynasty. Pitscottie wrote that, 'In the same zeir the king of Scotland bigit ane great schip, and maist of strength that ever sailed in Ingland or France'. This was the *Great Michael*, laid down in 1508, and one of the wonders of Europe. She represented James's dream of a large and powerful Scottish navy.

According to Pitscottie, the building of this mighty vessel stripped all the timber in Fife, and great shiploads of wood were imported from the Baltic. The cannons and other materials came from all over Europe, and construction began at Newhaven under the expert eye of M. Jacques Terrel, the King's Master Shipwright. She was two hundred and forty feet long, thirty feet broad, and her sides were ten feet of solid oak. The cost was over £30,000, and no expense was spared. Her chandeliers came from Belgium, as did the expensive lanterns which used polished horn instead of glass. The compasses were from Flanders, pitch and tar from Denmark, cordage and canvas from France, and tin and copper from Cornwall. She was designed to carry over six hundred sailors and gunners, and a thousand soldiers, and the English watched her construction with increasing anxiety.

The *Great Michael* was launched in 1511 amidst a blast of trumpets 'at the outputting of the kingis great schip', and the entire court gathered to watch her slip into the Forth. James

The *Great Michael*, one of the wonders of Europe, was built in 1508 by James IV as the flagship for Scotland's first navy. One of its shipwrights laid out its dimensions by means of ornamental ditches near the now vanished Tullibardine Castle.

ordered a cannon to be fired point-blank at her sides, but so strong were these that no damage was caused. When finally fitted out she made an impressive sight as she rode at anchor with her four great masts alive with banners and penants, and her huge poop and decorated forecastle towering above other craft. The whole country rejoiced with pride at the knowledge that a new era had arrived in Scotland, for as more and more warships joined the *Michael* the navy became a power to be reckoned with.

At the outbreak of the Flodden campaign the great fleet sailed proudly away to aid the French against the English, and so force Henry VIII to fight on two fronts. Alas, the ships were not under the skilful command of the veteran sea-dog Sir Andrew Wood, but had been given to the Earl of Arran, Hereditary High Admiral. For some inexplicable reason he decided to sail north, and a few weeks later arrived at Ayr. The furious king sent Sir Andrew Wood to assume command but it was too late.

On land James was forced into battle against the entire might of England, and, along with most of the Scottish nobility, he perished at Flodden Field. Ironically, a major cause of the defeat was lack of artillery, for the army had been stripped of its best gunners to man the warships. The mighty vessels vanished into oblivion after Flodden, and the *Great Michael* lay rotting at Brest only two years after building.

This is the story narrated by Pitscottie, and near the end of his account are the words, 'If any man doubt my words let him pass to the zeit [gate] of Tullibardine, and their affoir they samin he will zie the length and breid [breadth] of hir plantit with hawthorne by the wrightis that helped make her'.

It seems one of the master shipwrights employed on the *Great Michael* came from Tullibardine. When he returned on leave, the local people so pestered him for details that outside the west gate of the castle he dug deep ditches the width of the ship's sides, and shaped them to its exact length and breadth. They were lined with hawthorn trees, and filled with aquatic plants. Some of the hawthorns were still standing in 1837, and apparently the excavation itself was still visible in 1883.

Even though the castle no longer existed, I wondered if I could still find traces of this relic of Scotland's Golden Age. I returned to Tullibardine. There was no sign of such an excavation, but I thought an aerial photograph might show something. So it was back to Edinburgh, and the aerial photograph section of the National Museums. The staff found a photograph of the area and placed it in a machine which threw everything into three dimensional detail, but, despite a close scrutiny, we could see nothing.

I reasoned that if it was water-filled, then a stream probably fed it, but there was no water visible on modern maps. So it was off now to the Map Department of the National Library. Although nearly all published maps of Scotland are held here, I could not find a large-scale plan of Tullibardine any earlier than the nineteenth century. The staff looked up their references, and suggested that I try the Scottish Record Office, and there I went through their indices of old plans relating to Tullibardine, and found two that seemed promising. These were held in the Charter Room at Blair Castle and a photographer friend was, fortunately, going north on an assignment, so I arranged with the factor to have the plans laid out. My friend returned with some excellent prints of a plan of 1790 which showed a stream running near the castle. Now I had to relate this to my aerial photograph which was on a different scale. I photographed the modern map and enlarged the negative until it coincided with my new prints, and marked off the stream. Armed with this, I returned to Tullibardine and traced the underground stream until it ran into a natural wooded hollow. I wondered if this was the spot, but couldn't be certain and I prepared to abandon the whole idea.

Just before leaving for the last time I called at West Third Farm and enquired of the farmer and his wife. They could throw no light on the subject apart from pointing out a stone from the castle built into their house, and suggested I see a Mr. Maxtone, the retired factor, who lived in the hamlet of Tullibardine.

Mr. Maxtone was more than helpful. Yes, he knew the exact site, but there was now nothing to be seen apart from the odd hawthorn root dragged up by ploughing, and he indicated the spot on my map. It coincided perfectly with the route of my underground stream which must also have fed the moat. Mr. Maxtone went on to tell me of the Chair Tree which stands in the woods behind the site of the castle. This is a huge oak, over seven hundred years old, and in earlier times the lairds of Tullibardine had a platform built in its branches from which they watched contests of strength and skill taking place in an area below.

Innerpeffray Library, near Crieff, the oldest public library in Scotland.

With this fresh information I returned once more to Tullibardine, and found the Chair Tree, now gnarled and shorn of many of its branches, but the remains of an arena about twenty-five yards in diameter could still be seen. From here I went to a small marshy hollow, situated in a ploughed field, where the dimensions of the *Great Michael* had once been carved out of the ground. It symbolised a nation's new-found pride, and the dawning of a new age which was not to be, but, like the great ship itself, everything has now vanished into oblivion.

Innerpeffray Library

Near Tullibardine is Scotland's oldest public library containing a priceless collection of rare books. Oddly, this is not located in any of the major cities but is sited at the remote rural backwater of Innerpeffray, about four miles from Crieff on the B8062 to Auchterarder. A metalled track leads off this byway at a curious wrought-iron sign, and meanders a mile or so through open fields to the library building and the attached chapel of St. Mary's.

The library was founded in 1691 by David Drummond, 3rd Lord Madderty, who was an unusual man for his time, for he preferred the scholarly arts to those of war or political intrigue, the normal occupation for men of his rank. However, this did not prevent his taking up arms alongside his brother-in-law, the Great Montrose, at the Battle of Tibbermuir in 1644.

Before the conflict he was chosen to parley under a flag of truce with the opposing Covenanting forces, but his white flag was ignored and he was seized and imprisoned in Perth. Fortunately, Montrose won the day, and the following year Lord Madderty was released upon payment of 2,000 merks Scots. This salutary experience had its effect on him, and he devoted the rest of his life to study and learning. He married twice, and his second marriage to Lady Beatrix Graham, sister of Montrose, brought him a dowry of 20,000 merks which he partly used to start his collection of books.

Lord Madderty's castle still stands as a ruin by the banks of the River Earn, about half a mile south-east of Innerpeffray, and is a typical L-shaped fortified residence of three storeys. However, as it was built in 1610 when life was becoming more peaceful, it lacks the usual turrets and other defensive features. Although the ruin is still imposing, it is difficult to imagine that this was once one of Perthshire's finest mansions with long tree-lined avenues and pleasure gardens.

As Lord Madderty's life drew to an end he decided to establish a library for the education of the local community, and had the books which had given him so much pleasure moved from the castle to the Chapel of St. Mary's. Initially they were housed in a small gallery at the west end of the church, but later a small building was built in the graveyard to accommodate the overflow.

Four years later, in 1695, he died at the age of 84, leaving three daughters. In his will he directed that 6,000 merks be left in trust to Lord Carmichael and John Haldane of

Gleneagles to maintain the collection for the benefit of all. Unfortunately, a flaw in the will rendered it void, but Lord Madderty's heir and nephew, Viscount Strathallan, decided to honour his uncle's good intentions and vested 5,000 merks for the upkeep of the library and for the salaries of a schoolmaster and librarian.

The present building which houses the library was built in 1750 by a descendant, Robert Hay Drummond, Archbishop of York, who added many fine volumes of his own to the collection. It is a handsome, white structure attached to the old chapel of St. Mary's, and its well-proportioned first floor with its high windows looks out over rolling, fertile countryside. The site is a superb one, for the two buildings stand on a knoll overlooking the River Earn with magnificent views all around, and particularly to the north where the Perthshire mountains rise up behind Crieff.

The library itself is reached by a stone stair, and in the well-lit room the walls are lined with over 4,000 books varying in age and value. Many of them are priceless, and the more valuable and interesting are exhibited in glass cases.

There is a notable collection of Bibles, the oldest printed in Antwerp in 1530. This is the famous 'Treacle Bible', so called from the misprint in Jeremiah, chap. 8, v.22 — 'Is there no tryacle in Gylyad?' Also on show is the small Bible which was the 'Booke tyed on a rope' around the neck of the Great Montrose when he went to his execution at Edinburgh's Mercat Cross in 1650. It contains his signature, while many of the pages are filled with his comments and sketches, revealing the scholarly side of this great general. On one of the pages is found his immortal lines: 'He either fears his fate too much: Or his desert is small: Who dare not put it to the touch: To gain or lose it all'. Owing to the close family connection there are many other relics of Montrose.

Another notable Bible, the only one of its kind, is a copy of Marot and Bega's Psalms of 1567 with music printed with sol-fa lettering beside the notes. There is the 1541 sixth

Gravestone of the Faichney, or MacNaughten, family in the churchyard of St. Mary's, Innerpeffray, near Crieff. It depicts the two parents and their ten children.

edition of the Great Bible with a prologue by Archbishop Cranmer, while a Bible of 1602 has a footnote by an eighteenth-century Lord Madderty stating that he had begun to read it for the thirteenth time.

The oldest book in the library is Barclay's *Shipe of Follys* of 1508, while the finest example of sixteenth-century scottish printing is Hector Boece's *Hystory and Cronikalis of Scotland* of 1540. Other books of note include the first English translation of Virgil's *Aeneid* by Bishop Gavin Douglas (1550), the *Sylva Sylvanus* and *New Atlantis* by Francis Bacon, and *The History of the World* (1614) by Sir Walter Raleigh.

But surely the most unusual book is the *Hystorie of Four*

Footed Beastes by Edward Topsells (1607), which contains pictures and descriptions of animals never seen outside a nightmare. As befitted a rural community, there are many eighteenth-century books on agriculture and farming, including *The Farmer's Letters to the People of England*, which contains a strong condemnation of 'idleness, drunkeness and tea drinking'.

Of local interest is the borrowers' ledger dating back to 1747 which shows that not only students, schoolmasters and ministers studied here but that volumes of weighty content were taken out by masons, weavers and wrights. Also on show is the visitors' book which records the signatures of James Barrie and George Bernard Shaw who visited Innerpeffray within a few days of each other in 1924. Their names were written with a goose quill pen, still used by today's visitors, the annual gift of an anonymous benefactor.

Attached to the library building is the single-storied St Mary's Chapel, built in 1580 by Sir John Drummond, 1st Laird of Innerpeffray. It replaced a much older church, mentioned in 1342, and has been the burial place of the Drummond family since its foundation. Part of the previous church remains and a stair at the west end leads to the small gallery where Lord Madderty originally established the library.

The chapel is now under the protection of the Department of the Environment and was renovated some years ago. Unfortunately, it proved impossible to restore the superb frescoes on the walls and ceiling, although patches of these remain. Also around the walls are the coats of arms and tombstones of the various branches of the Drummond family, including the noble houses of Perth and Strathallan. Buried here too are Lord Madderty and his two wives. When a vault was opened here last century for the interment of the then Earl of Perth, there was found the skull of Allan of Moidart, Chief of Clanranald, who was buried here after being mortally wounded at the battle of Sheriffmuir. There was

Monument to the unknown Maggie Wall, executed as a witch at Dunning in 1657.

much puzzlement why his skull was split, but the reason for that was recounted in Chapter 6.

Surrounding the chapel is an ancient graveyard, for Innerpeffray was once the centre of a thriving community. A hamlet, famed for its annual Lady Fair, once nestled here below the Library where the Roman road north forded the Earn, and this later became the main highway to Perth. All has now disappeared, although many of the inhabitants lie at rest in the churchyard. The gravestones here are ornately carved and many are inscribed with trade insignia. The most unusual is the one marking the burial place of the Faichney or MacNaughten family, who came to Perthshire from Argyll to help the Drummonds win the battle of Knock Mary, and were given land in reward. Their stone depicts a man and wife and their ten children, and is said to have been carved by candlelight.

The soil of the churchyard is very fine, and is known to have been mixed with sand for several feet under the direction of the priests who appointed this task as penance for any moral transgressors.

From Auchterarder to the Ochils

Nearby Auchterarder is renowned as having the longest main street in Scotland, a fact used to advantage by James VI when he acquired the throne of England. A supercilious noble was remarking on the splendour of an English town which had several drawbridges. James replied he had a small Scottish burgh which had over fifty drawbridges, and this was just a village. The English court was immensely impressed, but James failed to add the 'drawbridges' were simply short planks of wood used by the inhabitants to cross the open sewers and burns which ran through the street. The town today has a relatively modern appearance, for it was burnt to the ground in 1715 by the retreating Jacobite army after the battle of Sheriffmuir.

Between Auchterarder and the Ochil Hills is a little-known but fascinating area, best explored by taking the Glen Devon road at the Gleneagles crossroad, then turning off at the side road marked Duchally. In the glen below is Gleneagle House of the Haldane family who have been associated with this area for seven hundred years. Their original castle, now ruined, stands on a nearby wooded hillock close to the twelfth-century Chapel of St Mungo, preserved as a family war memorial. From the latter derives the name of the famous hotel and golf courses, although more correctly this should be spelt Glean Eaglais — The Glen of the Church.

A mile or so further along the side road and the gaunt ruins of Kincardine Castle can be seen perched precariously above the gorge below. This was the principal seat of the noble family of Montrose and the residence of James Graham, the Great Montrose. He was possibly the only national commander who fully understood how to utilise the fickle Highland clans in major warfare and how to use their peculiar fighting habits to advantage. Not much of his castle remains for it was burned and levelled in 1646 by the notorious turncoat Middleton, acting under orders from the vindictive Archibald Campbell, Earl of Argyll.

The byway joins the B8062 and continues towards Dunning. On the right of the road is Tarnavie, the Ground of the Boat, and here a huge grassy mound can be seen in the shape of a Viking longship, the burial place of a sea-king who fell here during an overland raid. Shortly after this is a curious rough stone cross with the painted words, 'Maggie Wall burnt here as a witch, 1657'. It is curious there is no official record of her death. There was certainly an anti-witch mania here in the mid-seventeenth century, and there was a major trial of the witches and warlocks of nearby Glendevon. One wonders if her execution was so shameful that the clergy wished to forget it, or perhaps she was the victim of unofficial local action. Somebody local seems to know, for each year the sign is freshly painted and a wreath placed upon the monument with a card inscribed, 'In Memory of Maggie Wall, Burnt by the Church in the Name of Christianity'.

The land on either side is part of the ancient estate of Duncrub, scene of the battle in 946 when Duff and Calene fought each other for the Scottish throne. A standing stone on a nearby hillside marks the burial place of Dubdon, Maormer of Atholl, where he was struck down while fleeing, and the spot is still called Thanesfield.

For nearly six hundred years this estate has been owned by the Rollos of Duncrub, descended from a Dane called Eric Rollo, who settled in Normandy around 800 A.D. His descendants followed William the Conqueror, and came to Scotland in the time of David I. A crest and plaque at the entrance to a park in Dunning village were erected in 1946 by Lord Rollo to commemorate his family's 550-year association with the village. Dunning, situated at the foot of

Thorn tree planted in 1937 to commemorate the Coronation of George VI. It replaced the original one of 1715 after Dunning's burning by Highlanders.

Rossie Law with its huge, prehistoric fort, is an attractive little town with a modern appearance, for it too was burned in 1715. The only house left standing was that of the local miller who cunningly lit some damp straw, and the Highlanders ignored the building which already had thick smoke pouring from the windows. A thorn tree planted to commemorate the town's destruction survived until 1936, and a new one was planted the following year.

From the square at Dunning, fascinating roads branch off in all directions, particularly those heading east into the Ochils, and are rarely travelled by the visitor. Perhaps the most exciting road, with remarkable panoramic views, is that to Milnathort or to Glenfarg on the other side of the hills, for this ascends seven hundred feet in under a mile, then runs through deep, hidden valleys with twisting hairpin corners.

Almost every road or track around Dunning brings fresh discoveries in the shape of standing stones, Celtic crosses, hill forts, small castles and keeps, the latter belonging in times past to some of the oldest families in Scotland who had roots in this area, among them the Grahams, the Oliphants and the Belshes.

Nearby Forteviot was the site of the Pictish capital of the province of Fortrenn, and of the royal palace of the Pictish kings until 843 A.D. when the Picts were overcome by the invading Scots under Kenneth MacAlpine. King Kenneth, first ruler of a united Scotland, died here in 860 and his body was taken to Iona for burial. The palace continued as a residence of the Scottish monarchs until the time of MacBeth and Malcolm III, when it became a mere hunting lodge. The location is said to be on the mound just east of Forteviot, opposite the church. A carved arch from the palace and other Pictish carved stones are now in the National Museums in Edinburgh. Near the arched bridge over the River Earn is Milton or Milltown, where Duncan I, later killed by MacBeth, took a fancy to the miller's daughter, and 'Tuk and Chesyd that woman, To be his leman'. She gave birth to the king's illegitimate son who later became King Malcolm Canmore.

On the hillside above stands one of the finest carved, early Christian Celtic crosses. It also marks the site of the Battle of Dupplin in 1332 when the small army of the puppet king Edward Balliol defeated a much larger Scots army commanded by the Earl of Mar.

This is the fascination of Perthshire, that every area has a tale to tell, and these stories and traditions stretch from the Highlands to the Lowlands, from clan chiefs to feudal lords, and from prehistoric to more recent times. I have told just a few of the tales of Perthshire that I have found interesting. Hundreds more remain to be told.

Index

Note: bracketed figures refer to illustrations

Aberfeldy 69
Aberfoyle 99, 101, 102, 103, 106, 107, 110
  Fairy Hill 101, 102, 103, 104, 105, 106
  Old Church 101, 104
Achallader 63, 66
Adamnan 47, 48
Agricola, Gnaeus Julius 163
Amulree 69, 78, 79
Anderson, James 87, 88
Anderston Relief Church 151
Angles 39, 40
Antonine Wall 164
Appin Murder 98
Ardeonaig 16, 70
Ardmaddy Castle 70
Ardoch
  House 168, 169, 170
  Parish of 174
  Roman Fort at 163, 164, (165), 165, 166, 167, 168, 169, 170, (170), 171, 172, 173, (173), 174
Ardtalnaig 81
Argyle, Duke of 191
  Earl of 189, 203
Atholl
  Stewart Earls of 190
  Duke of 190
Auchmore 70, 71
Auchterarder 202

Balliol, Edward 205
Balloch Castle 52, 63, 65, 67
  Red Book of 79
Balquhidder 90, 91, 92, 93, 98, 100, 102, 128
  Old Kirk of 99, 100, 101
Bannockburn, Battle of 4, 13
Barcaldine 63
Barrie, James 200

Beheading Pit (64), 64
Beltane Rites 42, 55
Ben Dorain 39
  Lawers 29, 81, 82, (87), 88
Benderloch 63
Bernane Bell 2, 5, 6, 8, 9
Bessie Bell 181, 183, 184, 185, 186, 187, 188
  grave of (187)
Bhacain 33, (43), 56
Black Diamonds 109
Blackwood, John 124
Blair Castle 191
Blane, Saint 146
Bonaparte, Napoleon 110
Botany Bay 138
Breadalbane 61
Bridge of Balgie 47, 49, 154
Brig o' Turk 111
  Iron Eating Tree at (112), 112, 113
Britons 36, 37
Brown, George Douglas 161
Bruce, King David 49
  King Robert the 4
Buchanan, Janet, of Leny 22
Burns, Robert 153, 156, 185
Byrne, John 175, 181

Caddell, Robert 120
  Thomas 118, 119, 120, 122, 124
Cailleach, The (48), 55
Caithness, Sinclair Earls of 65
Caledonians 163, 164, 172
Callander 27, 29, 108, 110, 115, 126
  Old Kirk of 111
Cam Beul, Fergus
Camelon 163
Campbell
  Alexander (pistolmaker) 120, 121
  John (pistolmaker) 120, 121, 124

John (Milton Farm) 82
of Aberucehill & Kilbryde, Sir
Colin 66, 133, 160
of Breadalbane & Glenorchy 80
Colin 1st Laird 61, 62, 80
Duncan 2nd Laird 50, 62
Colin 3rd Laird 62
Grey Colin 6th Laird 51, 62, 63
Black Duncan 7th Laird 63, 64,
65
Katherine 17
John, 1st Earl of Breadalbane 65,
66, 67, (69), 81, 85
Duncan, Lord Ormelie 86
2nd Earl 67, 83, 86
3rd Earl 67, 83
4th Earl/1st Marquis 31, 67, 71,
77, 83
John, 5th Earl/2nd Marquis,
15th Laird 68, 76, 78, 82, 84, 86,
90, 91, 92
Gavin, 3rd Marquis 68, 69, 70,
72, 75, 85, 86, 88
Alma Graham, 3rd Marchioness
68, 70
Charles William, 9th Earl 70, 71,
85, 86, 87, 88
Armorer, 9th Countess 87
John Romer Boreland, 10th
Earl, 20th Laird 71, 85
of Carwhin 67, 85
of Fordy 101
of Glenfalloch 68, 85
of Glenlyon
Red Duncan 51, 52
Mad Colin 52, 53
Robert 53, 54, 56, 66
of Glenure, Colin 98
of Lawers
John 80
Sir James, 6th Laird 80
of Lochawe, Sir Duncan 61
of Mochaster, Sir Colin 101
Isobel 101
Camusvrachan 33
Canmore, King Malcolm 205
Carnban Castle 51, 53, 56
Carn na Marbh 48

Chesthill 54, 56
Chisholm 49, 50
Coigerach 2, 5, 9, 10, 11, 12, (15)
Colquhoun
of Luss, Sir John 189
The Appin Companions 80, 81
Cromlix 150, 152
Cromwell 21, 110, 168
Cumberland, Duke of 122, 148, 149,
150, 151

Dalriada 1, 13, 34, 36
David I 13, 147, 189
Dewar 3, 5, 10
Alexander 11
Archibald 11
Thomas Douglas Battersby 12
Dewars 2, 3, 4, 5, 10
Bernane 5, 6
Coigerach 3, 4, 5, 6, 9, 10, 11, 12
Fergy 5, 6
Mayne 4, 5
Meser 5, 6
Discher and Toyer 62
Doune 92, 114, 115, 116
Castle 116, (120)
pistols 116, 117, 118, 119, 120,
121, 122, 123, (123), 124, (126)
Lord 162
Drip Moss 129
Drummond
Agatha 125
David, 3rd Lord Madderty 197
Earl of Perth 175, 191
-Home, George 127, 128, 129,
130, 131, 132
James, Lord, 4th Earl of Perth
167
John, 1st Lord Innerpeffray 200
Margaret 146, 152
Patrick 167
Robert Hay, Archbishop of York
150, 152, 198
Drummond, Blair 125, 126, 127,
128, 130, 131
Safari Park 131, 132
Drummond Castle 144, 168, 170,
175

Drunkie House 111
Dull 47
Dumbarton Castle 110
Dunblane 100, 134, 138, 142, 145,
146, 147, 148, 149, 150, 151, 152, 153,
154, 156, 159, 162
  Allanbank House 149, (151), 152
  Balhaldie House at (146), 147
  bishops of 146
  Braeport 158, (161)
  Cathedral 145, 159, 160
  ghost army at 171, 172, 173, 174
  Jessie, the Flower of 152, 153,
  156, 157, 158, (161)
  Millrow 161
  Old Doune Road 148, 150
  plague pit 182, (183)
  Strathallan Lodging 152, (159)
  Tannahill Terrace 159
Duncan I 205
Dun Geal 43, 44
Dunning 203, 204, (204), 205
Dupplin Cross 205

Eden, Hon. Ronald 152
Edenbellie (91), 94
Edinample Castle 82
Ellanrayne Castle 16, 17, 20, 21

Faichney, tombstone (199), 201
Fairies 102, 103, 104, 106
Fairy Hill 101, 102, 103, 104, 105,
106
Feradach 1
Ferguson, Duncan 100
  Muckle Kate 111
Fergusson, John (Heather Jock)
132, 133, 134, 135, 136, 137, (137),
138, 139
Fergy 2
Fianna 33, 34, 35, 36, 37, 38, 40, 41,
42, 49
Fillan, Saint 1, 2, 3, 4, 8, 9, 12
Finlarig Castle 52, 62, 69, 70, 71
Fionn MacCumhaill 32, 34, 35, 37,
41, 42
Flanders Moss 131, 132
Fletcher 63

Fords of Frew 125, 148
Fortingall 37, 42, 44, 46, 48
Fortrenn 40

Gartmore 98, 124, 137
Gathering Stone 143
Gillefillain 13
Glassingall 160, 161
Glen Boltachan 14
  Cailleach 55
  Devon 203
  Dochart 2, 3, 5
  abbots of 13
  baillie of 5
  John de 13
  Lord of 4
  Ducket 95
  Eagles 202
  Falloch 36, 37, 95
  Finglas 112
  Lyon 32-42, 47, 49, 50, 51, 52, 60,
  128
  Ogle 88
  Orchy 84
  Quaich 77, 78, 84
  Strae 50, 51
  Tarken 19
Gloag, Andrew 175
  Helen 175-181
  Robert 180
Goldmine 90, 91, 92
Great Michael 191-195, (193)
Graham 137
  James Gillespie 161
  Robert, Rev. 103
  Thomas, General 185, 187
Graham of Drunkie 93
  of Duchray 103
  of Gartmore, Cunningham 137
  of Gartur 136
  of Killearn 92
  of Meiklewood 130
Gray, Mary 181-188

Hadrian, Emperor 164, 173
Hadrian's Wall 164, 165
Haldanes of Gleneagles 115, 198,
202

Haliburton, Hugh 73
Home, Henry, Lord Kames 97,
125, 132

Ibar, Bishop 1
Inchbuie 24, 28, 30, 31
Innerpeffray Library (196), 196-198
   St Mary's Chapel 200, 201
Innerwick 51, 54
Invernenty, Wester 92, 98
Invervar 54

James IV 4, 146, 192, 193, 194
James V 189
James VI 9, 64, 189
James VII 66

Kenmore 63, 67, 69, 81, 82, 84, 86,
91
Kennedy, James 76, 78
Kentigerna 1
Kerrowmore 49, 50
Key, Jean 92-99, (96)
Kidnapped 160
Kilbryde 133
   Castle 133, 160
Kilchurn Castle 61, 62, 71
Killin 23, 67, 71, 75, 80, 96
Kinbuck 159
   Moor of 142
Kincardine Castle 20, 202, 203
Kincardine in Menteith 132
Kinnell House 21, 22, 23, 31, 70, 71,
86, 87
Kippen Churchyard 97
Kippenross House 155
Kirk, Colin 103
   James 99
   Robert 99, 100, 101, 102, 103, 104,
   105, 106
Kirk Lane 128, 129, 130

Lanrick Castle 114, 115
Lawers 62, 80, 81
   church 81
   Lady of 31, 78-88
   house of (82)
Leys Farm 143

Lochaber 97
Loch Doine 92
   Earn (head) 14, 16, 17, (18), 19,
   20, 89, 90
   Katrine 108
   Lomond 95, 108
   Tay 16, 19, 20, 62, 81, 83, 84, 88,
   90, 91
   Voil 92
Lynedoch 183, 185, 186

MacAlpine, King Kenneth 205
Mac an abba 13, 31
MacArricher 128
Macbeth 91
MacDiarmid, Angus 89, 90
MacDonald
   of Clanranald 140, 145
   Dugall the Cruel, 6th chief 140
   Donald Mhic Domhail, 12th
   chief 140, 141, 142
   Ranald Mac Ailean Oig 141
   Allan Dearg, 13th chief 142, 144,
   200
   Reginald George, 20th chief 145
   of Glencoe 52, 53, 54, 64
MacDonnell of Glengarry 9, 143,
144
   Rev. Eneas 11
MacDougall, John of Lorn 49
   John (Sidi Magdoul) 179
McGregor/MacGregor, Clan 13,
50, 62, 63, 64, 65, 114, 125
McGregor's Oak 114, 115, (117)
   Leap 51
McGregor, Alexander Drummond
of Balhaldie 147
   Sir Evan John Murray, 18th
   chief 115
   Gregor McGregor of, 51, 52, 62
   Sir Gregor McGregor of, 23rd
   chief 115
   Sir James 50
McGregor, Colin 92, 93, 99
   Duncan 92, 93
   James Mhor 92, 93, 94, 95, 97
   Rob Roy 92

Robin Oig 92, 93, 94, 95, 96, 97, 98
Ronald 92, 93
MacIldowie 20
MacIvor 50
MacKay, Dr Norman 59
McKerracher, Duncan and John 54
Macnab, Angus of Innishewen 13
    Gilbert of Bovain, 1st chief 13
    Finlay of Bovain, 8th chief 14
    Finlay, 12th chief 17
    Iain Min 18, 19, 20
    Francis, 'The Great', 16th chief 21-30, (23)
    Archibald, 17th chief 27, 28, 30, 71
    Archibald Corrie, 22nd chief 17, 22, 31, 71, 87
    James, 23rd chief 31
MacRuari, Amie 140
MacTavish, James 73, 75
Machany Water 175
Malcolm III 205
Mansuteus 46
Mar, Earl of 192
Masonic Home, Royal Scottish 162
Meggernie Castle 53, (57), 60
    ghost of 56, 57, 58, 59
Meikle, George 127
Menzies, of Culdares 57
    Alexander, Lord of Glendochart 4
Methven 184
Mill of Steps 175, (178), 181
Mill of Torr 126, 130
Mills, Lint 67, 83
Milton Eonan 47
Montrose, The Great 197, 198, 202
    Highland Army 65, 80, 83, 99, 125, 182
Moray, 6th Earl of 116
    Bonnie Earl of 65
Morocco 176, 178, 179
    Scottish Empress of 175-181
Moss Lairds 124-132, (135)
    house (131)
Murdoch, Thomas 120, 121

Murray 189, 190
    Sir William of Tullibardine 189, 190
    Lord George 191
Muthill 118

Neish, Clan 14, 16, 17, 19, 20
Ness 14
Newton of Doune 121
Newton Stewart 187

Ochtertyre Moss 132

Paisley 152, 155, 158
Perth 182, 183, 184
Perth County, Ontario 77, 78
Philadelphia Experiment 105, 106
Pictland 1, 36, 37
Picts 36, 38, 41, 44, 49
Pitcairn, Major 122
Pitscottie, Robert Lindsay of 192
Plague 47, 48, 182, 183, 184
Pont, Timothy 160
Pontius Pilate 43, 44, 45, 46
Pubil 40
Punch 72

Raeburn, Sir Henry 29, 124
Ramoyle 147
Ramsay, Allan 185
Reith, John, Lord 162
Rigg, Diana 162
River Allan 163
    Almond 183, 184
    Dochart 1, 197, 201, 205
    Earn 191, 192, 197, 205
    Forth 124, 126, 128, 131
    Knaick 166
    Teith 116, 126
Robertson, John Logie 73, 75, 76
Rollo, of Duncrub 203
Roman Envoys 43, 44
    Forts 163-174
    Legions, IX Hispana (Unlucky Ninth) 173, 174
    Marching Camps 130, 164, 165, 172

Roads 130, 145
Roro 50
Ruskin, John 159

St Andrews 47
Scott, Sir Walter 103, 107, 108, 110, 123, 186
Scots Magazine 152, 153
Shaw, George Bernard 200
Sheriffmuir 140, 145
    Battle of 142, 143, 144, 202
    graves on 143
Sibbald, Sir Robert 168
Sidi Magdoul 179
Smith, Alexander and Thomas 160
    Sydney Goodsir 73
Smith Institute 161
Steuart, James 151
Stevenson, Robert Louis 160
Stewart of Appin 80, 98
    of Garth 43, 50
    of Lorn, Janet 62
Stirling of Ardoch, Col. Moray 170
    Sir William 169
    of Keir, Archibald 162
    David 162
    Margaret 80
    Col. William 162
Stirling, Dr James 138
Stirling 109, 115, 124, 125, 131, 149, 155
    Carse of 94, 124-131
    Castle of 131
Strathallan, Viscount 191, 198
Strathfillan 1, (3), 4
    church of 6, (7), 8

holy pool of 6, 7, (10)
    prior of 5
Strathyre 90
Stuart, Prince Charles Edward 121, 125, 145, 148
Suie 2, 5
Swan, Annie S. 77

Tannahill, Robert 152-159, (156)
Taymouth Castle 63, 67, 68, 69, 70, 73, (74), 78, 79, 82, 86
Testing Stones 33, (35), 38
Tigh na Bodach (48), 55
Tiorim, Castle 140, 142, 145
Tomnadaschan 90
Trossachs 110, 111
Tullibardine Castle 189, 191, 194, 195
    Chapel (190), 191
    lands of 195
    Earl of 56
    Marquis of 190, 191
Turnbull, Mrs Joyce 181
Tweedsmuir, Lord (John Buchan) 78, (79)

Verne, Jules (105), 107, 108, 109, 110
Victoria, Queen 68, 84, 111, 170
Virginia 188

Wade, General 166, 175
Wall, Maggie, the witch (201), 203
Weir, Tom 75
Wentz, W. Y. Evans 104